Dead Woman Dancing

Dead Woman Dancing
on Her Grave

Dead Woman Dancing

On Her Grave

Unstoppable

Doris Wellington

Dead Woman Dancing on Her Grave: Unstoppable
Doris Wellington © 2008-2023
Dwelling Places Worldwide, home of books and letters
By Doris Wellington
Georgia/USA

Unless otherwise noted
All scriptures are taken from King James Version of the Bible
Public Domain
First US Copyright printing, 2021
Kindle Direct Publishing
 USA
Available on Amazon.com and other online outlets

ISBN-13:978-0998150727

Cover Design
Nancy Bookhart

Dedication

I dedicate this work to my mother, Hattie Vance Wellington, with whom I shared a full life of mutual love, admiration, and joy for poetry. She not only taught me how to live; she showed me how to live with dignity and the pride of womanhood—that it doesn't matter how many times life knocks you down, you can get up dancing if you don't give up.

Mudd: I honor you for your invaluable gifts—earth life, unconditional love, nurture of soul, faith in God, freedom to dream, wings to fly, and the unbridled force of your determined resolve. This is your enduring legacy, which I don't take lightly.

You're home now…

I dedicate this book to women who have overcome and continue to overcome tremendous odds—resilient—steadfast—wholly determined to leave a legacy of a bold, determined warrior in the face of opposition.

Table of Content

Foreword—Nancy Wellington Bookhart, PhD

Introduction—Sharon Wellington Boone

Enigma of the Divine—12
Once upon a Dream I Danced—13-19
Dead Woman Dancing on Her Grave—20-41
Stop Shuffling and Dance—42
We Speak—43-44
Birthed by Miscontraception—45-55
The Vindication of Rachael's Travail—56-71
The Water Monologue—72-78
Indomitable—79
Sitdownhushyourmouthstandupandholler—80-88
September Reign—89
The 63rd Chronicle of Psalm—90-96
Rebirth—97-98
The Unveiling—99
Manifesto of Misinformed Womanhood— 100-112
Dancing in the Womb of Captivity—113-120
Prophetic Ink— 121-125
Dance of Anastasis—126-142
The Poet's Lair— 143-147
The Plan of Salvation—148-155
Praise Dancing Salvation—156-168
The Me That I Am—169-172

My Mocker's Lament—173-174
War Dance—175-181
Preaching Blu Woman Bluz—182-193
Letter to a White Girl—194-196
Something Beautiful Within—197-204
Category Undeclared—205-233
First I Am—234-237
Episodic Update: Do Not Post—238-255
Do Not Dance Until I AM Not Found—256--263
I Waltzed with God the Morning of Genesis—264-269
Where I Dare Enter—270-273
My Decree of I Amness—274
Woman--275
Dancing with HER—276-291
Declare Your New Beginning—292-93

Foreword
Nancy Wellington Bookhart, PhD

Art of the Divine

Doris Wellington, an artist philosopher in her own right, refuses the conventional inscriptions on her utterances. She staggers not in the darkness of such naming and categories of historical determinisms. Instead, she scales the walls of Reason and Logic, not seeking validation of her voice, but to leave deposits across portals to represent that all such voices are as diverse and pertinent as the orations of Aristotle. To this end, she moves into these veiled realms as seer and orator, philosopher and artist, prophet and priest, and poetic, lyrical diviner of the invisible—not only daring to approach that which thought unapproachable, but moving in and out of the spaces of the divine and sacred to the phenomenon of the profane, as if to link these two agencies, separated by conversion of what was once sacred and divine for both; friends not foes; workers together in the travail of nature to cast a greater human species—the genius spirit, aesthetics as equilibrium; a symphony I have witnessed in the work of the author over years of collaboration and partnership in the arts. As poet, she is as raw, passionate, genuine, infectious, and fearless in her work as all prophets who dare aspire to transform worlds by the very nature of their vocation, which she approaches without trepidation, or restrictive mores that censor, disqualify or scoff at her gift as having no substance in reality, or her claims that this gift transports her between worlds held by most as imaginary and aren't by any means of human will or effort achievable; except, in (creative) partnership with God.

She is not occupied in the concatenation of the two worlds, not towards a mutual understanding, not even to become one with them, but so that they may confront the other in their absolute, their infinity, their grandiose design, and that we will behold them, equally enigmatic as all spheres of knowledge.

This enlightened woman of letters weaves the metaphysics and phenomenology in a tapestry of hope for all who dare cross the chasm to heed her voice and to experience the endowment of her gift. Deep within this artist is the birthing of the aesthetic as "art of the divine."

Introduction

I am the Legacy of a Woman
Sharon Wellington
Excerpt: Stokestown: Dreaming behind Closed Doors
Dedicated to Mudd

I can tell you a myriad of stories with images of handmade suits, dresses and hard-pressed hair and the snapshots a mother takes to remember the beginning—of hard-earned money sacrificed for orthopedic shoes and long rides on the bus sitting next to a woman wearing a well-tailored skirt and high-heeled shoes in route to clean those fancy houses—those three- and four-story mansions. But instead, I give you my fondest memory of a woman treading close to two feet of snow to go to work in a famous little town in Virginia. And I say, "think of this." As I watched through the screen door, I followed her bundled image down the porch stairs, out the gate, and as she trundled down the sidewalk, until she disappeared at the end of the block and all that was left was the last image.

It is an image that overshadows even more pleasant images of chocolate cakes, fried fish and ribbons that match the yellow dress. It is the image of a sharecropper turned domestic. And maybe for me it is a metaphor for strength—for the purpose that burrows through roadblocks, for the meaning that redefines a moment of inertia. Maybe for me it is significant to understand. And I am grateful when her love, loyalty to family, work ethic and commitment to faith rose in me when I needed it most, and to that to my daughters as a gift to be cherished. I am delighted that her charm and elegance appeared when I felt mine most insignificant. It is the gift of creation—God's creation, that we often view with ambivalence—that often puzzles us, and so we rot, often in the tomb of our uncertainty...waiting.

So, this is the greatest thing I remember...the legacy to walk while listening, to run while waiting, to race to become. This is what I remember most. This is the legacy I take with me from my mother, Hattie Mae Vance Wellington, just the simple, immeasurable optimism of a woman who "does" (with no motive higher than love—the love of God—the love of family—the love of humanity).

Enigma of the Divine

God pulled me from the depths of seas
I washed ashore
At summer's end
Bound to a scale
An ancient book
And a pen
I came as a voice
Fully endowed
Defying logic
And disbelief
To inspire
Enigmatic searching
Empower impotent dreams
And human longing
Using every gift
To affect change
Belabored
Perhaps burdened
By what I'd seen
Beyond the eyes
Of earthen beings
I drank from the fountain
That flows endlessly
From God
I am the Enigma of the Divine
Denied and reclaimed
In the bodies of others

Doris Wellington

Once upon a Dream I Danced
December 6, 2017

I dreamed I was a dream waiting
lifting soul and spirit
soaring above barren seas
and futures abandoned
and now I ask
where is it?
amid shattered ruins
and scattered remnants
I fondled the possibilities
when is a dream not a dream
and is it ever isn't

a flickering ember
from the smoldering heap
spoke to my disquiet
a dream unclaimed
is still a dream
it just needs a heart
to guide it

Dead Woman Dancing on Her Grave

In a moment of silence
I caressed the thought
Is a thing unfinished
considered naught
or can the windblown relics
of a broken dream
live again
if given new wings

how does one gather
from places unknown
a million broken pieces
now lost
the tiny flickering ember
from the ashen heap
consoled my despair

A dream that ever was
still is
It just needs new life
to grasp

Doris Wellington

I had a dream once
of uniting the world
with songs of peace
and healing
A dream so vast
and vociferous
even today it stalks me

Can a dream survive
the vicissitudes of life
and rancor of hell
and still
the flame of hope
yet glimmers
amid its will to live

the squished tiny ember
held its own
and proclaimed to my doubting
a dream thought languishing
never dies
it just waits
its rightful hour

Dead Woman Dancing on Her Grave

O 'to dream
A beautiful thought
imagine a
masterful vision
can such seeds
be aborted
in the womb
of infertility
when does that
which the dreamer imagines
becomes larger
than the dreamer
and alas
summons the universe
to inspire
another student

the dying ember
drew its breath
and whispered to the air
a dream deferred
is still a dream
born
and reborn
somewhere

The great and small
pass along
spewing
their human opinions
such a thing
has never been done
none has even attempted

while the ember
faded
into ashen ruins
mouthing
its last bequeaths
its will
and testimony
fold into me
take my hand
possess me
body
soul
and spirit

Dead Woman Dancing on Her Grave

Whether you
or them
or neither nor
someone
someday
somehow
the thing that I have
yearned so long
is suddenly resurrected

A child not tempered
by its fears
a stranger seeking
asylum
a loser thought unhinged
by life
will lift me from these ashes

Will I
a perfectly formed dream
refuse that hand
in marriage
just because
it doesn't come
wrapped
in ceremony

Doris Wellington

Invisible now
the fading ember
beckoned with its light
I'll take this one
The time has come
fill her with my fire

Hang on
never a dream
has been fulfilled
without the toil of night
without the weighty presence
of the soul's disquiet
pensive
pondering
preoccupation
quitting a million times

Never a dream has been fulfilled
without the will to fight
or the extraordinary
resilience
that runs through humankind
pregnant
with weary
watchfulness
waiting
for its time

~~Dead Woman Dancing on Her Grave~~

They declared
You are the offspring
Of the Immortal Spirit
Your hair is your glory
And your roots will replenish

But when they knew my strength
They conspired to dispossess me
Blot out my name in history
And auction my birthright
Piece by piece

They fattened their children
From my breast
Defiled the blood of my innocence
Until all that was left
Were the scattered remnants
Of a dead woman's bones

Then they closed the book
And forbade me to mourn my legacy

Doris Wellington

So
I shaved my head
And renounced my grief
And lay naked and barren
In the wilderness
Presumed dead

Life entombed in a makeshift grave
Inviting contempt
Bereaved of song

Womb in mourning
For generations lost
Or so
They thought

Four hundred years
I wallowed in death
And all the living
Wallowed with me
Weeping
And bewailing my despair

Dead Woman Dancing on Her Grave

I have come to this mountain
After a long searching
After an imperfect
And tempestuous turning

Years ago
I drank from the Rock

Purged
With water from The Brook

Washed away the stench of death
Then I waltzed with God
On the eve of deliverance

Some know my comings
My journeying up
From under the warfare
Typical of the hell
That thrust me into a darkness
That hid my sorrow
Like the veil

You Wonder

How I made it
From the hind part
Of inferiority
And why
My back is not bent
My head is not bowed
And why my spirit
Is still not broken
From sufferings
Inflicted upon my soul

You wonder
Why cotton sacks
Burlap strong
And the clinging albatross
Of a nation's scorn
Have not weighed me down

Why attacks of panic
And the threat of demons
In pursuit of my sanity
Have not bequeathed me the fate
Of polishing trophies
I never won
On the "No Visitor's Block"
Of the Prozac Ward

Dead Woman Dancing on Her Grave

You look at me
Inquisitively
Knowing the history of my slavery
My fight for survival
And dignity
And you wonder
How dominated
And dispossessed
My will supplanted every test

How it is
That my chin is erect
My shoulders squared
And my eyes once a fountain
Now fix themselves
Upon a dream deferred
Until now

You wonder
Why am I not dead
From discrimination
Miscegenation
Social incarceration

Or the systemic labeling
Most likely to fail

Or perhaps heartbreak
A less conspicuous demise
From stooping too low
Or bowing too long
To mortals
Who thought themselves God

Or from weary nights of insomnia
Stalked by self-pity and loneliness
Wondering
When it would be my time

But how
Is the question
That lingers most
In the thoughts of those
Who know me best
Or
Not at all

How still I rise

Against such odds
Defies reasoning and intellect
In most gambling minds
I shouldn't be here

Dead Woman Dancing on Her Grave

For my options failed
Before I arrived
And I became a byword
Banished to infamy
A proverbial mishap
A footnote inconsequential to life—
Mammy
Nanny
Blackie
Wench

Until now…

Now
I have them googling my name
How the hell I climbed out
Of the muck and mire
Of the nethermost
To emerge
The winner I am
Seizing the moment
Emphatically declared
From a heap of rubbish

Years rejected
And relegated to invisible

How stripped of identity
And left for dung
On a dark forsaken path
Where a bold
False prophesy hung

Do not Enter—

Dead woman down
Victim
~~Cannot~~ be
Resurrected
Too much to overcome

People
Take me seriously
Let me authenticate my credentials
I am a force to be reckoned with
The impetus of hope
Rising from the ashes of obscurity
And sepulchers
Sworn to keep me bound

I am dusk
Revisited as dawn
Seven times stronger
Impregnable

Dead Woman Dancing on Her Grave

My strength is linked to infallibility
I cannot fail

My energy flows
From infinity to infinity
Where there is no ebbing tide
No fate that binds

I am the daughter of eternity
I gave birth to divinity
Nine months cradled in my loins
I conceived and nurtured
God In flesh

When you passed me
You passed the pulse
Of humankind
Kicked to the curbside of Lo-debar

Polluted
You thought
In my own blood
Suffocating
In my own bowels
Plunging
To the farthermost
Of a pluvial grave

Doris Wellington

Wretched
Abysmal
But still alive

Sustained
By a thousand sunrises
Upon my brow
And a prophetic word
That refused to die

When I saw you polluted
In your own blood
I said unto you
Daughter
Rise

Clothed with invincible faith
To hide my shame
I bathed in the river Potentate
Ingested life undefiled
And incomprehensible
Rushing
From the cistern of perpetuity
To empower my rise
And steady my feet
For resurrection dancing
And the turning of my captivity
To laughter

Dead Woman Dancing on Her Grave

I am a celebration
Summoned by the velocity
Of the wind's breath
Upon my time
To reinhabit the uterus
Of hope
Reborn

Like the travail of winter
To bring forth
The healing of the ground

I am the soil
Of generations still coming,
The salt of nature's replenishing

I am sage
Seaweed
Sycamore
Cypress
Cedar
Bristlecone pine
Ginseng
Aloe
Vera
Yellow root wine

Doris Wellington

Rock incarnate
Metamorphic quartz
The quintessential balance
Of malignant and benign

I am the feminine force
Of the spirit God
Transplanted
From the brain center
Of power
Eons incubating
In a primordial loam

Until now

When I am summoned
From the ruins
And the ravages
Of the abandoned

To emancipate sons
And daughters
Forgotten

I am vanguard
Of the new millennium
The first and only
Mother of Eden

Dead Woman Dancing on Her Grave

Emerging from the carnage
Of Henrietta Marie
To reclaim the voice
Of my identity

Henceforth
You are forbidden
To ever judge me again
By the arch in my hip
The dimple in my chin
The texture
or length of my hair
Or the color of my skin

Do not Judge me
By the twitch of my brow
My Rubenesque breast
The Barbie ideal
Or the size of my dress
By the flirt in my smile
The strut in my stride
Or whether my locks
Are weaved
Wigged
Or dyed

Doris Wellington

Marvel if you must
Over my musicality
But mark me by my rise
Because when I'm in motion
I know no
bounds……………………………………………………………………

I am the fluorescent laughter
Of a Technicolor dream
Airborne
An opera over Venus
The flight of the Trumpeter Swan
A symphonic poem
Rising to the choreographed adulations
Of the Most High

I am the unruled
Unbridled rhythm
Of a Praise House
The soul of a Negro freedom song
A cross breed of the Harlem Renaissance
And an African drum call
Unscripted
Uncensored
Undefined

Dead Woman Dancing on Her Grave

I am a postwar apparition
Left for dead
Buried in ignominy
Raised in kaleidoscopic flesh
Above the ridicule of the oppressor
And the scorn of the oppressed
Above political conspiracies
And social indignities

Rising above
Bastard
Washer woman
Pickaninny
And Negress

I am now possessed by the purpose
That birthed me in this moment
To rewrite history
Towering over incident
Gathering and scattering
The spoil of my wrath
Bold
Unflinching
Stanchion

Immured in one body
One spirit
One defining victory
For those who came before

Doris Wellington

And when I arrived
I took the scroll
And found the place
Where we had been denied

And I danced
In the volume
Of the book
For a woman buried alive

Danced joy
Weightier
Then life or death
Regret or remorse
Danced out loud
Louder than the travail
Of babies
Ripped from my breast

I danced
In the midst
Of edicts and oracles
Charged to keep me bound

Danced words
Unquenchable
Like fire
Shut up
In the bosom
Of the soul

Dead Woman Dancing on Her Grave

Resonate
Unctuous
Full of song

Danced

For Harriet Tubman
Sojourner Truth
Sally Hemings
And McLeod–Bethune

For Dorothy Height
Phillis Wheatley
Ida B. Wells and
And Kara Walker

I danced like a butterfly
Abreast the moon

For Zora Neale Hurston
And Lena Horne
Hattie McDaniel
And Queen Mother Moore
For Bessie Smith
Josephine Baker
Billie Holiday
And Moms Mabley

For Rosa Parks
And Winnie Mandela
Shirley Chisholm
And Marian Anderson

I Danced
For daughters
Stolen from the womb
Never to become women
Their light diffused

Cynthia Wesley
Addie Mae Collins
Denise McNair and
Carole Robertson

Danced...
For Fannie Lou Hamer
Mamie Till
Miss Jane Pittman and
Women of the veil

I Soared
In the essence
Of my being
For Evers
Shabazz
And Coretta Scott King

Dead Woman Dancing on Her Grave

For Mary Louise Smith
And Claudette Colvin
Hattie Vance Wellington
And Grandma Rosa

Crazy danced
For Sarah Baartman
And Nannie Helen Burroughs
Jarena Lee
And Ella Fitzgerald

For Lois Mailou Jones
And Madame C J Walker
Augusta Savage
And Marian Shields Robinson
For Fanny Kemble
And Gwendolyn Brooks
Angela Davis
And Ingrid Jonker

For the Motherland
And Ntsiki Biko
For children in the loins
Of the Diaspora

Doris Wellington

I danced
For ages of being told
I couldn't
Shouldn't
Dance at all

Danced
For Colored men and Negro boys
African kings
And queens deposed
In the belly of the Atlantic

Danced
For America's
Women of black
Too strong to be broken
Too proud to forget

Danced
With almighty God I Am
Who delivered our song
Glorious again

Danced
In the temple of my doom
Eternal oblation
Forever whole

Dead Woman Dancing on Her Grave

I danced

And danced

And danced

And danced

'Til redemptive rain
Cleansed my soul
And I forgave
Their every wound

'Til enemies repented
For their sins
Praised my strength
To their chagrin

'Til laughter crowned
My despair

And the ancestors bowed
To declare
My song

Until the host of heaven
Stood in awe
To etch my story
In the book
Of Hebrews Eleven

Behold a woman
Bound in chains
Snatched her headstone
From its place
Left her fetters
Neatly laid
And danced
On her grave

Stop Shuffling Along and Dance

So
Hold your head up not down
Wear your shoulder square not round
Pick your feet up off the ground
Walk like you're going somewhere

Lift your chin to the clouds
Move with purpose in your stride
Pick your feet up off the ground
Walk like you're going somewhere

Stop your shuffling along
Incline your ear to your soul
Pick your feet up off the ground
Walk like you're going somewhere

Speak a word to your resolve
Faith shall keep my dream alive
Pick your feet up off the ground
Dance
You're almost there

Doris Wellington

We Speak
Excerpt/Rebirth of Womanhood—1995

They said, "speak not"
And we were silent
Submissive
Incensed with self-pity
And rage
Voices mute
Future distorted
On blank pages of a history
Never written

They said, "speak now"
And we spoke then
Permissive outbursts
Fostered by secrets
And unspoken lamentations
Fettered to the nakedness of soul

They said "speak this"
And that we spoke
Fearful
Censored
Verbal silence

Dead Woman Dancing on Her Grave

They said speak "woman"
But we spoke life
Proverbial wisdom
Conceived in experiences
Hidden in the womb of time

They hated our words
Warning us
"Speak no more"
Threatening to drive us back
To the prison of the unheard

In protest
We regurgitated our contempt
For warriors scorned
And declared
Our unwavering resolve

To speak
High and lofty words
Reverberating
Through the pages of the past
Telling our stories
Writing our own history
Forging our own future
In our own words

Doris Wellington

Birthed by Miscontraception

A contradiction
No such act
Can exist deliberately
Yet I'm the evidence

Hidden
In conception
Intentionally
Imposed
To prevent my existence
Birth controlled
By social devices
Divisive
Mortally inflicted crisis

Every attempt to keep me back
Thwarted
Injustice miscarried
And I'm delivered
No less a woman

Dead Woman Dancing on Her Grave

Fisted
Clenching
The blood sweat spoil
Of victory
No plot could foil me
No plan could abort me
You might not applaud my strength
But you must acknowledge my existence

Strip me of everything
Born by death
My luscious lips
My swivel hips
Eyes that gesture
Sensuality
Take away my kinky locks
My twists and braids
Or my fried and dyed
Flowing
Anything

That identifies the container
That carried my soul
Away from Africa
In the body of the ancestors

And still
I will defy
Any misinformed
Woman
European
Or African
Who believes
She can pump her lips
Fill her breast with silicone

And extract booty
From artificial
Unknown sources

And tans the excess of body
Swinging black babies
Bought by wealth
Or birthed by
Miscontraception
Miscegenation or
Miscarriages of DNA
Revisited as love

Black bodies
Sweat mingled with blood
Flowing from hatred
And greed
Ebony sweat

Black as the deepest recesses
In the dark of the coal mines
Or the dense caves

Pregnant with the land's
Opulent resources

Call me Colored
Or Negroid
Mock the thickness of my skin
The round of my breast
My full lips
And colorful style
Then inwardly desire
What God so freely gave

Deny me the right
To learn your language
So that I will not rise to defend
Your bigotry
And I will arrogantly protest
And give you Euladah

Doris Wellington

Indoctrinate me
With your godless religion
That subordinates to slavery
And drives love
To the remotest indignities
That the soul can render

And my spirit will still soar
Above the Kilimanjaro
Like Nelson Mandela

Call me pickaninny
Wrench
Boy
Lazy
Unteachable

Whip me until my veins
Explode
And I bleed purple pride
That speak to the strength
Of my grandfathers
Lacerate my skin
Past the pigmentation
And display my body
In your museums of mockery

Dead Woman Dancing on Her Grave

Refute my intelligence
In the Bell Curve
Or my humanness
In Plessy vs. Ferguson
Or Brown vs. the Board of Education
And I will still give you
Thurgood Marshall
Willie Gary
And Johnnie Cochran
Harriet
Sojourner
And Madame C J Walker

Cast my children
Upon your altars
Of poverty
I made me black children
While feeding yours
From my breast
They call me Nana
Nanny
And Sally Hemings
But they are as much mine
As they are yours

And when you raise them up
To be my master
They will call me
Nana under their breath

Doris Wellington

Withold
Land to invest in
Houses to live
To cover the indignity of homeless
And the hope of dreaming

Sabotage my right to a fair trial
Quash motions for retrial
Create laws that lock me out
Mark me with smear campaigns
Of drug lies and drug lords
Or
Lock me away
For a felony conviction
When you know fool well
It was just a misdemeanor

Kill me just because
I wear a hoodie
While walking black
In a gated community
You think you own
Stop and frisk me
Profile me
While Harris and Klebold
Terrorize to haunting

Defame
Misname
Disown me

Deny me a Small Business Loan
Raise the credit score
To keep me reaching
But never acquiring
Refuse to raise
The minimum wage
To keep me begging
For welfare
And ~~reparations~~
Always trailing
In the census

And still
I will rise
The legacy of a woman
Mother Africa bore
From the loins of God
Transported me
Across the chasm
Of the earthborn

And
Carried me strong
Upon the backbone of the land

Sand squishing through bare feet
Head carrying the food of nations
Loins pregnant with kings
And princes
Queens
Who will reign

Until the King returns
To claim
The land that thrust me
Into the lap of destiny
Who burned the chaff of wickedness
Who kidnapped
Me bound in chains
Across the Atlantic
With no compass
Of balance
Between here and there

I am no slave

Dead Woman Dancing on Her Grave

Give me no fallow glimpse
Of hope
And I will seize the reigns
Declare mutiny upon
Waters of despair

I will do what my nature does best
I will fight

And even if you manage
To sell me to the highest bidder
Upon auction blocks
Strewn with the blood
Of the innocent
Rip my babies
From the breast
And carve your prejudice
Into their memory

Still…
They will regurgitate
Indifference
And apathy
To become

Doris Wellington

Sojourners of Truth
Frederick Douglass
Harriet Tubman
And Martin Luther King, Jr.

Tie up my womb
In unholy tampering
With nature
Try to abort my legacy
Hang my children like fruit
From trees that
Smell like the autumn husk
That burst wide
Like rotted melons

Still

I thrive

Birthed by miscontraception
Born in captivity
Wrestling in the womb
To overcome
Like Jacob
I take dominion over those
Who deplore my existence
Because chains can't bind
The mind of the free

The Vindication
of Rachael's Travail

Today I wept in the face of the past
Wept
For the mean and mindless
And less than grateful
For those who live for evil
Or die hating
Wept for failures
I cannot fix
With zero desire
To go backwards
To try

Today
I wept
For reasons
I thought resolved
In evolution
Of soul

Wept...
For sins I thought
Washed away
Forgiven
And forgotten
Absolved in atonement
In blood rites for sinners
Made righteous

Except
They visit me today
Bold
And vociferous

But mostly
I cry
Because I have no children
None to stand before my bed
When dying comes
To pass my legacy on

I ask...
The muffled moans
Caught between
Sleep and wake
And dreams
I can't decipher

Dead Woman Dancing on Her Grave

Is this the fruit
That I have borne
Is this my karma
For secret scorn
What divine privilege
Did I mistake
As my sacred human right

My womb has born no heir
And I weep for children
I did not have

Not because of barrenness
For I am far from that
But for the fellowship
Of flesh and blood

I question
Whether God
Or life
Thought it fitting
Or fair
That from among
Women earth born of woman
I am among those
Who did not bear

If for sins against the womb
My seed has been divinely consumed
I must respectfully ask
Why?

If all unrighteousness is sin
Is there lesser
Or greater offense

One yields the harvest of rape
A boy child from a date
That should've never been

Yet nature takes her in arm
And she gives birth
To a child

Others parade their sex appeal
Before endless suitors
And lovers then
Birth daughters

Some desire to abort
But can't
Or don't
For one reason or another

Dead Woman Dancing on Her Grave

Even bad mothers conceive
Mad
Insane mothers
Carry seed
Partying
Drinking
Drugging and
Smoking
Or prostituting
Mindless abusing
Of the body

No consideration
For children
Still
They deliver
Casting aside the born
Like afterbirth
Or garbage that interferes
With living
Boasting and parading
Like ragdolls
Adding to the scourge
of the living

Doris Wellington

I on the other hand
Committed none of these
Against my uterus
Or scorned the thought
Of bearing children

Yet I feel deprived
Truth hugs my despair
More are the children
Of the desolate
Than the married with wife

And Jesus retorts
On the way to Calvary
Weep not for me
But for yourselves
And the children you will bear

Now I stand
In blessedness
For children withheld
From the breast
Barren of fruit
And milk that nurse
And regurgitates reverse travail

Dead Woman Dancing on Her Grave

I bore no child
To walk this earth
Or cried the tears
Of a mother's pain
Who learn her child has been slain
Or born dead

After nine months carrying
Her bundle of hope
Claimed
Named
And held
For one eternal moment
Of goodbye
Now lifeless

I've never waited by the phone
For a child
That would never come home
And I would never know why

I've been spared the test
Of raising boys without dads
And have no word to compensate
For their loss

I've not withstood the devil's wrath
Resisting against blood
To save my child

No child of mine has raised a hand
To strike me down
For the sin of neglect
Never been called a Bitch
Or hoped to die
By the mouth I fed
And proudly kissed

I will never know how it is to love
Sons turned daughters
Or daughters turned sons
The hope of grandchildren
Lost in knowing
They are still worthy
Of my love

I will never wail
For loss of child
To crack
Meth
Or heroine
Alcohol
Or domestic violence

Or a soldier Missing in Action
Prisoner of War
Or died in action
For their country

Or a child
Who couldn't take his pain
Put the gun to her he
And pulled the trigger
or cast herself downward
To death
Whether God or life
I've been spared

I'll never know
How to love
Those
Born crippled
Or handicapped
With maladies and diseases
That can't be cured
By any medicine
Or know the miracle
That answered my prayer
For their healing

Doris Wellington

I'll never experience
a child

Ravaged by cancer
Muscles collapsed
Never to walk
Crawl
Or skip
Never to speak the heart
Held in silence
Lips stammer
And I answer with hugs

I will never know
Children born
Traitors
Rapists
Haters of country
Serial killers
And mass murders

Pedophiles
Peace breakers
Gangsters
And thugs
Terrorists
Heathens
And scum of the earth

Dead Woman Dancing on Her Grave

I am spared
Baby mama drama
Or dead-beat dads
Or jealous wives
Just because
I am mama

Yes
my earth womb is empty
And my milk dried up
But I have never known
Nor ever will
Experience the pangs
Of reverse travail

Beneficiary
In the back of a hearse
Dead prematurely
Bathed in grief
Overtaken by sorrow
That can't be nursed
Inconsolable

Thank God
I will never birth
A Stalin or Hitler
And regrettably
Not a Nelson Mandela

My womb will never be tainted
By a serial killer
An Idi Amin
Or Jack the Ripper
Not an Imelda Marcos
Or a Susan Smith
A Heinrich Himmler
Or Cynthia Alvarez

It will be spared forever
A son or daughter
Who while I sleep
Murder me for insurance
Or to get what they believe is theirs
By birthright evil
Take the life of the one
who bore them gladly here

A Michael Wayne Jackson
Will never be my shame
Neither a Josef Fritzls
Or Exondia Salado

Dead Woman Dancing on Her Grave

Father
Forgive me
I'd never considered
How blessed I am
Having born no children
And still they rise
To call me blessed
From North to South
And from East
to West

So
I will not be sorry
When I watch from heaven
How those who remain
Read my journey
There will be no regrets
No desire to do over
What I totally surrendered
In the discharge of faith
I shall not cry for more worlds
To conquer
More souls to save
More children to leave
To be stalked by Satan

Doris Wellington

I will live my best life now
Love as much as I'm allowed
Even when love is not returned
In the measure I desire
Surrendering what others
Dare to sacrifice
The love of husband
The quiver of children
The famish of soul
For the fullness of spirit

The honor of man
In the declaration
Of heroism
Serving in places
Where there are no eyes
No ears
No lips to give homage
Of love rendered
No plaques
To bear the names earth given
No shout outs
For not quitting
No robes to adorn
Educational achievements

Dead Woman Dancing on Her Grave

What then will I have lived for
How will I be remembered
What postscript
Will be placed
upon my existence

Let it be spoken
Among motherless children
Whispered by the homeless
And imprisoned
By widows and widowers
Who walked alone

Those whose spirits were lifted
In songs
In secret words of comfort
Of food given to famish of soul
And body
Or just the gesture of a smile

The laying on of hands
The burden of life made easy
In a unexpected gift
Garments that covered
 Naked surrender
 A coat to warm
 Against the toil of winter

Doris Wellington

Let it be said of God
That when no one was listening
All the windows and shades
Were closed against me
When my cupboard was bare
And my bank account empty
I bore the Kingdom
Strong sons and daughters
Carrying faith to the end of my journey
A mother

The Water Monologue

Refusing to travel barren
I bore spiritual children
Laid spiritual bricks
Upon eternal buildings
Some will miss it
All together resist IT
~~But there's no greater dream~~
~~No grander plan~~
Than to live this life honoring God

Even nature suffers
When I'm not assured of who I am
The earth trembles in rejoicing
When I walk certain
Of my path
When in me
God lives
Moves
In manifest dominion

God lives
In the abundant overflow
Of a thousand years
Cast from the waters
That bore my name
~~No test rivals who I am~~

Doris Wellington

I rise from the sea
Of a million crystal waves
Staking my claim

As water
Carving paths through rocks
Tunneling through mountains

If trapped
I create new paths
By the force of my being
And the strength of my presence
I enter and exit
Like none other
Saturating
Consuming
Purifying

In power tempered
By the Source
That nourishes the harvest
Replenishes draught
Quenches thirst
Brings the wrath of storms
Breaks barriers
Balances the fury of fire

Inhabiting every element
Of nature
Frozen black invisible to the eye

Mysterious virtue that heaps upon banks
Clarifying fluidity poured from heaven
Frigid to the touch

Lighthearted tear drops
Thunderous applause
Transparent
Rising from beneath
A S C E N D I N G
Covering the terrain
Obscuring vision
Nebulous

I am Water
Refreshing
Incubating life
Baptizing the soul
Into spiritual renewal
Healing
And cleansing the body
To whole
Expressing the soul's
Emotions
Removing the stain of toil
In garments of flesh

My eyes transparent
To the depths
That thrust me forward
A fountain
Where others drink
From rivers of life
Flowing out of me
Running through me
Filling to abundance

Connecting nations
Harnessed to create energy
Forcing to the surface
Toxic debris
That threatens contamination
The great force
Of nature
Without which life would wither
And die in the womb
And on the vines of reproduction

I am Water

Dead Woman Dancing on Her Grave

I run to overtake destiny
Fire consumes it in its rage
But water balances the scales
Of fire and rain
Working in covenant with blood
As witnesses to the divine
On earth
Healing the land

Absorbing the vengeance
Of the wrath of God
Destroying iron
A thousand years standing

Truth be told
I've never been without child
I am water
And I have given birth to the cryptic
And hidden
In tens of thousands dreams and visions
I've nurtured a millennium
Of songs
Poems and unspoken lyrics
Words flow from me
Like a rushing tempest
From the River Niger

Before one sentence punctuates
Another overtakes it
Like twins fighting in the womb
For exit
I am never without child
I have birthed the consolation of nations
Mediated peace in families
Comforted the solitary
In the 5th Chronicles of Songues
From my own bosom

I am water

An eternity in the womb of God
But here in earth boundaries
I flow in limited measures
But when I'm done with this assignment
When every drop of life
From me has fallen
When there aren't souls left to water
No thirst and hunger to quench
From spiritual draught
Or starving

Dead Woman Dancing on Her Grave

When I've cried the last time
For children I did not birth
To drink endless from the belly of God
When no one else needs a breakthrough
And all paths have been sealed
Against me
Then
My children
Birthed from the River
Flowing from my spirit
Shall serenade my homeward

When I shall no longer yearn
The fellowship of children
Whose seed I didn't carry or
Supply the balance of water
To quench the thirst of the wayward
Until the then of that time…

I am water

Doris Wellington

Indomitable
Excerpt from the Rebirth of Womanhood/1995

Who is it who seeks to break me
Dispossess me of my soul
Which long ago was broken
By troubles never lived by those
Who pursues my strength
In vain

Dead Woman Dancing on Her Grave

Sitdownhushyourmouthstandupandholler
Song of Hands and Feet

If these feet could talk
Or these hands speak
They would tell a story
That only journeyers
Can appreciate
Feet would converse with hands
"Do you remember when?"
In the way that only
They can
Laughing dance
Joyful claps
Stomping and praising

Feet stomping
Hopscotch
Jump rope praise
Feet tested to cramping of legs
And hands

Walking in the heat of sun
For children's bread
Or protesting injustice

Doris Wellington

Declaring
I might be feet
But I know where I've been

Track the miles
That knotted my knees
And swelled my ankles
Like the purple cabbage
Or red bell pepper

I've sat down and gotten up
And sat down again
For there was no rest
I leaned right-handed
Against a fence
The doorpost
Or steadied a bench
With hands just as jaded
Snapping fingers closed
To abate pain
Running wild
Through my soles

Dead Woman Dancing on Her Grave

If I could speak
I would talk feet code
Sit me down
Your impulsiveness depletes my core
Leaves me defenseless
And challenges my strength

If it were not for our
Connected mission
I would easily shut you down
Cut off the circulation
To your mindlessness

You waltz
Without restoring me

You've left me chaff
Dehydrated of moisture
Barren of electrolytes
That replenish to
High stepping joy

My nails are brittle and broken
Ingrown
And ugly from neglect
I need a pedicure
Like the manicure
You worship

Doris Wellington

Bath me in aloes
And honey
Massage my agreeableness
To accompany you
Without respect
To thorns and thistles
Along highways
And hedges
Pour sweet oils
Into a basin
And let me hear
Your feet song

I stepped in the water
The water was cold
It chilled my body
But not my soles

I beat the devil running
But I'm so tired
Lord
Plant my feet
On higher ground

Clad me in comfortable wear
And not fashion
That distorts the template
Of bone

Dead Woman Dancing on Her Grave

Or cramps to delirium
My joy
Grace joy
That dances on the altar
In feet clapping love songs
Take the fetters off my feet
So
I can dance
If these feet could talk
They would yield to hands
That wave in frantic
Or somber retreat
For feet that have quit

Hands that hail a taxi
To relieve sweat
Pouring down the pant legs
To ankles

Hands that war in worship
Despite
Calluses and corns
And swollen bunions

Blistered and sore
From too tight boots
Or too long
Standing or walking
To and fro
In gainful employment

Doris Wellington

Speak hands speak
Clap from your pores
Pour from your clap
Clasped in anxiety
And despair
But raise no flag
Of defeat
Hold captive no remorse
Paint your nails
In kaleidoscopic shades
Adorn your fingers gold
And your wrist with bangled jewels

Exfoliate deadness
That dulls the skin's natural
Radiance
And hide youth behind stories
Only the hand can tell

Speak hands
Of cotton picking
Bean pulling
Putting in tobacco strong
Jack rocks
Jump rope
Double Dutch turning

Dead Woman Dancing on Her Grave

Stitching hems 'til dark
Scrubbing clothes
On the old tin board
In an iron sable pot

Rolling dough
Cutting collards
Wiping noses
And backsides
Preach hands preach!
Of whipping nights
Children inclined to disobey
Despite meals
Placed gingerly at tables
Spread with delicate love
Pleasurable to the pallet

And water drawn
For the basking of body
Refreshing from storms
And tempestuous life
Then lifted in prayer
To God who sends his answer
In new strength
For another day

Doris Wellington

If these feet could talk
Or these hands speak
They would thank the other
For the harmony of hearts
Working collaboratively
To pull or push along
Those who could not
Live without the stories we tell
Doing what we do everyday
Without acknowledgement

Bodies distorted by disease
Stature stunted by growth
Heart heavy with pain
Eyes swelled with grief
But feet don't fail me now

I've got miles to go before I sleep
Words swell in my throat
Because nobody knows
The cross I bear

Dead Woman Dancing on Her Grave

But even though words
Come slow
I raise my hand
And pat my feet
To tell my story

Girl…
Don't be weary in well doing
We got you
Nobody need know
How tired we are
So

Sitdownhushyourmouthstandupandholler!

Doris Wellington

September Reign

I take the crown
From summer's reign
Passing through its final stage
I am September

I am the harvest moon
The reaper's plow
I am summer's sunset
September's child

Neither heat nor cold can shatter me
I survive in bitter frost or
Under scorching rays
I am September

I am the dusk of a dawn
Ushering in scene three of nature changing
I am the voice declaring the sunrise
Of a new day
I am September

The 63rd Chronicle of Songues
September 26, 2014

I lay in veiled sorrow
Waiting my time
She quenched my thirst with blood wine
The water that held captive
My desire for earth life
One morsel of dry bread fed my hope
As she consumed the scraps leftover
Walking estranged
From her mother's prayer
A burlap sack swings loosely about her waist
I quickened
Precipitously
She stopped like a work horse
Whose reigns had alerted its driver
Of impending danger
Loose blades of grass
Brushed against her bare legs
The snake slithered across her path
Thinking it did so
incognito

Doris Wellington

She cradled her fears
And held one steady
Unflinching gaze
Defying the prophesy of old wives' fables
One fleeting moment of contemplation
Held her captive

She gingerly stroked the top of her belly
If it were true
Her child would be cursed
To crawling
Defiant
Obstinate hope
Kicked in the womb
And the enemy
Lusting for prey
But detecting none
Slid across the summer grass

        Victimless

Dead Woman Dancing on Her Grave

In two months
She would deliver me
And we would meet again
Amid the scourge of dehydration
And I would live again
upon my knees
Past the age that children walk

She would carry me
Until beneath
Became repulsive
And I decided to rise
And stand upon my feet
To defy once again
The halfwit prophecy
That hinged upon fear

Revisiting
Clinging
Like the albatross of a dream

Aborted

I would rise and walk
And demand my vengeance
For all those who fell victim
To the method and myths of deception

There will be nowhere you can hide
I will see you in the dark
Cunning
And in the light of the scriptures
I will find you
Cowering behind ignominy

In dreams and visions
I will discern your motives
And unravel your strategies
In fasting and praying
I will pursue you
Relentless

Through the land of earthborn strangeness
Until your ambition to conquer me
Spoils your harvest
Like fruit that hangs too long
Upon infested vines

And fields that die before
Farmers can gather their seedlings
I will join the ranks of the forgiven
Whose sins you can never
Hold captive
Or demand their allegiance
Your children will spew you like bile
In rituals and rites of salvation

Dead Woman Dancing on Her Grave

They will renounce you
And sever the ancestral blood ties
Of those who ignorantly
Welcome and
Worship
Your lies

Our hate will be mutually full
With nowhere to store the excess
Except upon the battlefield
Of enemies

Using tried and tested
Methods of seduction
You will seek to entice me
With dreams of power
Prosperity
And the praise of deceitful
Inglorious splendor

And for a second of contemplation
One fleeting moment of maybe
 I will negotiate the price
 And find it too exorbitant

Doris Wellington

I will have no master
For even God declined my invitation
To bind my soul to his
Choosing rather
I conquer it with the power
Bestowed
In resurrection
You will offer pomp
And grandiose ideas
Unachievable
And I will leave you
Without a prisoner
As did my mother

Sixty-three years
Of Septembers past
I will hunger
So you will not feed me
I will thirst
And refuse your quenching

I will walk alone
So as not to require your company
And I will dance without a partner
To reject your pity
Among the jubilant feet
Of the oppressed

Dead Woman Dancing on Her Grave

I will endure hardship
As a good soldier
And I will decline
Your arsenal of weapons

I will wound and bleed
But I will not suffocate from blood
Sustained in battle
I will die

So you can't kill me
And I will rise with Him
To repudiate your boastings
Then I will incline my ear
To the rafters of heaven

And there
Amid testimonies
Of warriors
Who eluded your capture
You came
And found nothing in us
At last
We walk
Without the fear of stumbling
We stand
Without the fear of falling
But until then
I am not for sale

Doris Wellington

The Rebirth of Womanhood

I am God's purpose
Personified
Reborn in earth
A forethought
I am with God
In the beginning of creation
And the unveiling of Glory
In humankind

I am one of them
To receive the commission
Of joint-heirs
Over creation
The inheritance of God
When they were commanded
Be fruitful and multiply
Fill the earth
And have dominion
I am there

Dead Woman Dancing on Her Grave

I am not
And never was
In God's hand an empty urn
Undefined
From ancient of days
Until then
I've always reveled in Zoe life
Fulfilled

Then cunningly
Dispossessed
Naked and aware
I Died
Yet there I am
In God's mind
When He redeems
His magnum opus
From the fall
Now restored to Godly glory
I give birth to victorious
 Again

I am the seed of life
Extracted from the loins of greatness
Don't take me lightly
Or handle me without sacred regard
For my destiny
I am Woman
Enigma of the divine

Doris Wellington

The Unveiling

Planted in me are works of praise
All concealed in an earthen grave
Love potent but unshared
Victories desired but not dared
Dreams inspired but not pursued
Cures discovered but not used
And a myriad of other things
Lying dormant inside of me
Songs penned but unsung
Art created but not hung
Paths found but not travelled
Nations conceived but not delivered
I dare not die before you see
The harvest of good hidden in me
For I must return unto the tree
The fruit of the seed sown in me

Manifesto of Misinformed Womanhood

I am not a manikin
Manipulated
For the eye
Dressed and staged
For window shopping

Alluring to the lust
Of soul
Bereft of substance
And human emotions
Dragged and carted off
Between promotions
Discarded when usefulness
Is determined over

I am sober
Holy
Crowned with glory

I am not some inanimate object
Turned on for cameras
Clicked off for editing
Valuable only
When others are benefiting

A mere machine
Porous and clogged
From lack of attention
And proper care
Fondled only
For the satisfaction
Of selfish motives
And lascivious pleasures
Then stored
In a dark room
Like negatives
Being processed
Or in plain sight
For public inspection
Or curiosity
Tampering with that
Which is not broken
To flaunt skill
In the presence of an apprentice
Who looks on and longs
To know
But neither has passion to learn
Nor skill
Of which to boast

Dead Woman Dancing on Her Grave

I am not a blank canvas
Erased
And painted over
By the stroke of a brush
Or the whim of genius

Regardless of how inspired
The artist boasts

Not an empty urn
Filled with dead woman's ashes
Not fragile glass
To be handled
Disdainfully

Not a bag of bones
Without sense ability

I am woman
Skin and blood

Woman
Marrow and bone
Woman
Tissue and cartilage
Woman
Sinews and spleen
Woman
Arteries and veins
Woman

Doris Wellington

Prick me and I will bleed
Punch me
And I will swell
Bend me hard enough
I might break

Abuse my labor
And I wane tired
Wear thin of strength
Die
Prematurely

I am woman
Feelings and emotions
Woman

Mind and will
Woman

Break my heart
And it will emote pain
Abandon me to scorn
And I will grieve
Reject my children
And I will bleed endless tears
Of hate and revenge
Hate and revenge
On steroids

Dead Woman Dancing on Her Grave

Deny my rights
And I will blaze a trail
Of righteous indignation
Upon the pages
Of your history
And dance
My victory loud

Disrespect my opinion
And reap the wrath
Of my vengeance
In undeniable success

But I am more than emotions
More than
The intellect of reasoning
Woman
More than
The power of choice
Woman

Or
The will to dream
Multi-faceted
Multi-tasking
Woman

Doris Wellington

I am
The creative genius of God
Woman
Building a nation
On the backbone
Of faith
And the wings of prayer
Woman

I am a spiritual force
Made in the image of God
Woman
Created to reign
Woman

Endowed with God purpose
And power
Compassionate and Giving
Woman

Long suffering
And temperate
Woman
Faithful and committed
Woman

Dead Woman Dancing on Her Grave

Mission-minded
And selfless living
Woman

Forgiving and forgetting
Woman
Not one shaped
by religious
brainwashing
for the sins of Eve

If I disobey
By choices made
I fall from grace
If I live in sin
Shaped by iniquity
I stagger in darkness

If I rebel against truth
I lose my spiritual center
And fall back
To infinitesimal

Walking in the shadows
Waiting to be captured
By an Adam not coming

I am more than
A lyrical bridge
To a romantic encounter
Or a one-night stand
That leaves the DNA
Of a love child
Worshipped
Given up for adoption
Or abused and neglected

More than a selected ringtone
That seduces into compromising
Positions
Or abandoned principles

More than the wining and dining
Of indifference
The half-hearted commitment
Of marriage

More than a love note
Tucked under the pillow
To suffice for time
Not given

Or conversation
Not rendered

Dead Woman Dancing on Her Grave

More than the annual
Valentine
Or Birthday
Giving
That fades a minute after
Midnight
Christmas
And resurfaces
In a New Year's Day Repentance

Signed

Sorry
CHARLIE
JOHN
LEVI
FRANK
JASON
JR
GEORGE
MONTAE

I'm more than that…
I am more
Than a flick date
Or a late-night trip to the club
Bathing in the stench
Of mediocrity
And make do living

With someone who doesn't care
That I am loyal
To one earth man
Husband
Friend
Soul mate

I love adorning myself
Strutting my stuff
Respectfully

But
I'm more than contact lenses
That dazzle the eyes
Or stilettos that lift the posture
Of the buttocks
More than weaves and dye
Highlights and mascara
And disposables
That must be repeated
To enhance what is not

I refuse to allow
What could never define me
Bind me
Determine my worth
Or set my standards

Dead Woman Dancing on Her Grave

I am woman born
Woman strong
Woman
The pride of husband
The boast of children

But more than that…

I am my Father's song
Sung in every language
And in every hue
And tone
Words drafted
From my divinity

I am the book
Written by grace
The front cover
That bears God's name
Author and Finisher
Of my faith

The words flow evenly
Upon the page
Then unevenly they fall
God picks me up
One fragmented phrase
At a time

Doris Wellington

Then gingerly
Smooths the edges

God
Without You
I'm nothing more
Than
A Dangling
Participle
A cliché
A metaphoric rendering
Incomplete
A figure of speech
Inconsequential to context
Synergy
Or rhyme

A mere façade
Hiding everything I despise

Life punctuated
By ambiguities
And exclamation marks

Dead Woman Dancing on Her Grave

OMG!

Repeatedly

I stumble

Ensnared again

By the same fault

A run-on sentence
Not knowing where to stop

Except for the author's craft
I would be labeled
Or discarded
A proverbial mishap

But I'm constantly
Revised
And edited
Until the content
Reflects
Who I really am

Doris Wellington

Dancing in the Womb of Captivity
July 29, 2016

I do not know
If I were a writer born
If the writer birthed me
Or I birthed the writer
Despite all the tattled
Tangled life I'd been given
Whether the light summoned me
Or I summoned its
Metaphoric cover
To hide the shame of my existence

Born in the midst of dismal
And disdainful odds
Stacked beyond the reach of living
Ice crusted dreams
From a barren icebox
Without the possibilities
Of food that nurtures growth

From month to month
Waiting government assistance
Of dried parched
Grains
And rice

Block Cheese
And powdered eggs
Inside gray battle cans
Labeled to restrict the poor
US Department of Agriculture
Not for Resale

I tore the box around the cheese
And scribbled my dream
Light years removed
From where I slept
Still I
Wrote
Words that flowed
Like the water
I was denied for bathing
And cooking
And savoring
To refresh the stench of toil

Like water
I caressed the words
Holding captive
The image
Of the hope
They promised

Doris Wellington

"An Aspiration"
I wrote
"Out of inspiration
Deprived
A journey that
Only the strong survives"
I was but a child

What did I know
Of dreams and aspirations
Hope and determination

Still
I wrote
"The Little Black Rose"
Grows alone on the vine
Pushed aside
By those seeking a rose of yore

Whimsical
Proud
In her allure
No one had ever seen such
A departure from red

And yet
A rose by any other color
Is still a rose
Lift your full budded ebony pose
Among the clones
Little Black Rose
Fairer
Fairest
Among all

Where did the words come from
With their comforting
Their power
To ensnare the soul
In the place
Where lack had no rival

Except the literary cloak
Born amid the scourge
of survival
Allegorically
Mystically
And profoundly
Ambiguous
Where I hid my misery
And my fantasies

Doris Wellington

There is no bread
On the table
No meat among twelve
No pleasantries
Except the voice of the keeper
Of dreams
Spreading her enthusiasm
And casting her spell

Banana Pudding is coming
At the end of tobacco
And roasted chicken
With dumplings
Corn bread
And collards

Keeping our desires aflame
With the image of tomorrow
In the meanwhile
I wrote
Borrowing from the sonnets
Of Elizabeth Barrett Browning

But how had she entered my world
Where she and Shakespeare
Collided upon the same course
To mentor me
Through a portal in time

How had Rudyard Kipling
And Phillis Wheatley
Langston Hughes
And James Weldon Johnson
Entered my existence

How had Edgar Allan Poe
And William Cullen Bryant
Penetrated the veil of my despair
Bursting forth
In kaleidoscopic dreams

And conversations held sacred
Between those
Who weave their narratives
To create eyes
In places where there is no vision

Sojourner Truth
Kahlil Gibran
Solomon
Paul Lawrence Dunbar
David the Psalmist
Emily Dickinson
The Bronte Sisters and
Walt Whitman

Doris Wellington

There is no money
For school pictures
Or new shoes
To replace those worn
By the elements
Of nature
No ice cream soda pops
Just snow cream at Christmas
You just have to be patient

Sugar syrup
And stove top fritters
And the delusion
Of dinner will have to do
For now

I gently unwrapped
The loose-leaf papers
And poured my soul
Onto the pages
I scribbled
April 1965 across the top
For reasons
I never knew
Just me being
eternally optimistic

Dead Woman Dancing on Her Grave

That one day
This place will testify
In my defense
I did not die
Among the scorned
I was reborn

Amalgamated
With revolutionized minds
That held one common thread
To destiny
Write as deeply
As you can breathe

Ingest life and death complete
Then regurgitate indifference
So that no force binds your soul
To mediocrity
Write…

And so, I did
At fourteen
Not knowing
Where the concept of love festered
In heart or spirit

1965 is my witness
Of the language of love

Doris Wellington

Prophetic Ink
July 28, 2015

Dear Father
You have given me
The syncopation of rhyme
I am poetry
That flows freely like water
Unconfined
But never discomfited
Going where water goes
Doing what water does
Breaking down
Breaking through
Gushing forth
I can no more be restrained
Than water is dry
Or controlled by dictates
That do not lend themselves
To the power of my being
Like
Iambic
Pentameter
Limerick
Ballad

Dead Woman Dancing on Her Grave

I am
Past stanza and stage
Act or scene
Couplet
Or meters
Strung across the page
To be deciphered
Or not
By some literary novice
In conflict with my style
Judging the depth
And breadth
Of who I am
Commanding
Allegories
Metonymies
Similes
Or lack thereof

Or an Oxymoron
Or aphorisms
That obscure the real
In hyperboles
Or wisdom
Wrapped in fables
Analogous

Doris Wellington

I am none of these

And all these combined

The river that flows the course
Of all exaggerated
Or real
The rule
And the exception
Pseudonym
Antonym
Homonym
Farce
Synonym
Euphony
Appositive

Assonance
Cacophony
Atmosphere
Tone
Parable
And paradox
Myth
And metaphor

Dead Woman Dancing on Her Grave

I am the narrative
That flows through the vein
Of truth and lore
Of all poetic force

Never confined by the dictates
Of orthodoxy
Or conventions
That unteach

And bring into captivity
The exploration of self
Building
And rebuilding
Without deviation
From the norm
Applauding sameness
Rejecting the expression
Of what cannot be explained
By the status quo

The masters
Of enslavement
Of mind

Doris Wellington

I am one of them
Still searching for the path
To free myself
From Shakespeare
Edgar Allan Poe

Elizabeth Barrett Browning
And Edith Warhol

I am none of them
And all of them combined

Langston Hughes
Phillis Wheatley
Maria Polydouri
Paul Lawrence Dunbar
Emily Dickinson
Rudyard Kipling
Solomon the Great
Robert Frost
William Butler Yeats
Plato
Socrates
Aristotle
Euripides
and Maria Zambrano

The Dance of Anastasis

Can You Guess My Age
I have fought wars
No one my age should have fought
And won
Civil war and civil rights
The revolutionary struggle
For identity
In these United States

I have been held captive
By the dreams
Of the sharecroppers
Labor sold to the highest bidder
Putting in tobacco
Pulling cucumbers
Picking cotton at four cents a pound
Just to pay the rent
To live in a shotgun house
One more month
Exposed to the indignities of poverty

Doris Wellington

I've been hungry
More times
Than I care to remember
Eating black eyes
Without seasoning

Evicted for no reason
Except
I was just one too many
Undesirables
I've walked to school
In shoes too tight
Baby toes exposed by holes
Cut to fit the feet
Attacked by the elements
Frozen stiff by winter's breath
Unsympathetic

Do you know what it's like
To wear grown up clothes at ten
Made for women who wear perfume
And bras
And girdles to hide
The bulging of years

Dead Woman Dancing on Her Grave

When all you want
Is to be looked at
Like boys look at girls
Who wear clothes their age
Instead
I wore a backward blouse
To cover the shame of life
Bequeathed to those
Deemed
Less likely to succeed

Those who know their worth
But rarely given the chance
To contemplate the future
Cause they are too busy
Overcoming
What others take for granted

Clean water
A hot meal
A roof that does not leak
Bed springs
That don't bite
Floors open to critters
And crawlers

Doris Wellington

A working toilet
Or paper goods
Instead of cornhusk
Or grocery bags

Have you ever combed the stench
Of somebody's trash
To find something
To feed upon
Or eaten candy you found
On the ground

Or clay dirt
And ice cubes
As a delusionary substitute
For food
To stop the pang of hunger
Or the pain of disease

To long one moment of heat
That fills the cold damp of
Winter
Or one cool moment
To cover one sundrenched day

Dead Woman Dancing on Her Grave

I've seen the hopes of mothers
Dashed from diagnosis
Of incurable diseases
Children nothing more
Than a medical experiment
Or a mishap of science
Or nature
Like a polluted landscape
Disappears behind the horror
Of a tsunami

That sweeps whole cities
Into its arms
And carry them away
To places unknown

Or hurricanes
That devour the earth's terrain
And leave
Whole nations
Uninhabitable
Never to be the same

I've seen fathers
Pleading to be spared for children
But their pleas go deaf
Behind the blast of evildoers

Doris Wellington

hold hostage
For sinister plans they enjoy
At the expense of innocence

I've been spat on
Buked and scorned
Talked about just because
My hair cascade below my buttocks
Because I'm smart
And my eyes twinkle when I talk
I'm not a loose woman
When I love
It's one man
Whole

I don't fool around
Or present my body
Unholy to dogs

My skin is darker
Than yours
My gender leaves question marks
In people's journals
My weight exceeds
the acceptable norm

Dead Woman Dancing on Her Grave

My IQ is below 100
And I have mental
And emotional challenges
I might not ever conquer

Because my politics differ
From yours
And my bank account is not
Flush with wealth

I have health issues
That lock me out of insurance
Or assures that I will always
Be a victim of circumstances
I cannot afford

Do you know what it's like
To want to die and can't
For there's no reasoning
To lead the way
Or you fear
That death will come too slow
Or too fast

And you'll live to hear it
Everybody's thoughts
That you were not even old enough to die

Doris Wellington

Guess what
How old do you have to be
To have two lives
That interface
Two faces to face
Two deaths to die

I can't even guess my age
For if I am as old as I have lived
If there is a year that marks
The deepness of pain
For every heartache

A year goes by
Then I am ageless
As the love that anchors
The endless joy

Springing from eternal waters
Never depleted by time
Recyclable

Summoned fresh
Like rain
To cover the deepest sorrow

Dead Woman Dancing on Her Grave

To push back the veil of heartache
And beckons laughter
Laughter that conceals
A multitude
Of missed opportunities
To mourn

Laughter…
Soaring with eagles
Sauntering like peacocks
Rising and falling

Swelling full
Like the wind
Blowing
Boisterous
Untamed laughter
That even age can't defy

Cyclical laughter
Carried on the backbone of slaves
Like African mothers
Bore nations
Without the honor of kings

Doris Wellington

Laughing
Miscarrying seed
From stress
And restless toil
Still laughing
Defying the odds

Staring her in the face
Generations laugh in her womb
Until delivered
And princes will be crowned kings

And she will laugh
Until she burst wide with pain
Stomach tied in knots
For joy
And sadness in one refrain
For her man child is now a king
Of war
And her strength
Bows but does not break
For she is the mother of a nation
Now buried in decay
Age defined by what remains

Dead Woman Dancing on Her Grave

I too am a king
Birthed from the loins
of the King of kings
No earth king compares
His crown is untarnished
No earth children mourn him
For he lives forever
There are no shrines erected
To console those who weep

I am his temple
I worship at His feet
He lives inside of me
His garment
Secures me against the torment of fear
He holds me fast
In his bosom
Where I sleep
Until night gives way to dawn

Weeping hushed
Behind the crescendo of the promise
Of another day
To lean the full weight of faith
On Him
Infallible

Doris Wellington

Long before Martin Luther King
Became the symbol of civil rights
Before he planted one foot before the other
To march through the south
In search of a freedom
God born

Long before he wrote
From the Birmingham Jail
Before Bloody Sunday
On the Edmund Pettus Bridge
Or the March on Washington
In swelling numbers

Dropped like water
No discriminating color
Of the toil

That held men together
Like brothers
Swept by the tide of destiny
An eternity before
White mothers
Locked arms with black mothers

Or humanity hoisted their children
Upon their shoulders
To view hatred clad
Behind white sheets
And masked

Dogs biting at the heels of children
Kings swaying in the ambivalence
Of the future
Coretta and Martin
Yolanda and Dexter
Bernice
And Martin Luther King, Jr III

Blood running through the cracks of cement
Encrusted
To bear witness
Fifty years and counting
I was then
In the moment of hovering captivity
Born and birth
From the loins of a King
Who took my agony to the cross
And sealed my future
The legacy of a dynasty
Impenetrable
I have no delusion about this country
No misconceptions about freedom

Or the disenfranchisement of hope
That incarcerates the dream
Of those
Freer when they knew
They were but slaves

Than now
When some hold
Some distorted idea
Of Abraham Lincoln
And the Emancipation
Proclamation

I bear witness to a King
Who some will say
Is part and parcel of the same
American farce

Still
I beg to disagree

Massa didn't teach me to read
Or hand me over
Reparation seeds
To fuel my dream
No National Law
Granted me the will to live
Or the courage to die
Nor write the writ of success
With me in mind

No president
Stood and called me out
From the ditches and gullies
Of suicide

No Constitutional Bill of Rights
Empowered my rise
From death to life
Or granted restitution
Of ancestors' blood
That no man could reclaim
Irrespective of promises

Then responding to the Gospel
They had defiled and distorted
For gain
Praying that God
Had to be greater

I offered myself to him
A vessel
Believing without a doubt
I could be saved
That I could forgive
Their murdering ways
Their socio-pathetic
Devious character

Their pedophilic lust
For children
The greed that stole honest labor
The rape of a land
To buy their future

If I could without a doubt forgive
Without becoming a slave
to remembering
If I could wake each morning
And still feel human
Dismiss my desire
To seek vengeance
Or spew my hate
Against their children

Then I have risen
To a plain that marks true freedom
Redefines greatness
Defies all reason

No earth king heralded
From either side of the Atlantic
Neither the Motherland
Or Atlanta of America
Grants such shifting of life
That binds the heart to laughter

Dead Woman Dancing on Her Grave

And births from seeds of human failure
An immeasurable depth
Of hope redeemed
I am not the daughter
Of human error

I am the Legacy of a King
Ageless to time
Bearing the weight of all my years
In one act of grace
That leaves spectators to wonder
Why I don't look
Like where I've been

Doris Wellington

The Poet's Lair

I am the art of divine speculation
Standing five feet almost three inches
I've earned the difference
Walking tall
In the footsteps of angels
Immersed in a truth
Borrowed
From experiences
Walking with God
God walking with me
Through the valley of lurking shadows
Death howling at every juncture

For those who thought me dead
I'm still alive
Dancing unafraid
In the midst of fire
Across a vigil grave
Where mourners
Who once wept my demise
Now dance with me
That which God bore
Lives again

Dead Woman Dancing on Her Grave

I am a work of enduring art
That hangs in the gallery
Beyond this realm

My value will never diminish
For I've been tested and tried
For authenticity
And found to be an original
Indigenous
Never counterfeit
Or carbon copy
Not cloned to any one's rhythm
I am the soundtrack
Aboriginal

One marvel
Manifested
From a seed sown
In earth brown
Upon the sands of Africa
And bore across
An uncertain timeline
To the trumpeting
Of natives
Who witnessed
My citizenship

My portfolio swells with God's favor
I receive in generous portions
Through dreams and visions
What others labor to achieve

Two-hundred themes for movies
One hundred manuscripts to books waiting
Three-hundred sermons and songs
Delivered to the solace
Whose harps once hung
Upon willows

Still
I am not obese
For as soon as I am full
I empty myself into hearts that wait

Angels follow me around the world
Protecting my spirit from strangers
While my body lies
Suspended between
Here and there
Discerning where I am
Earth or heaven
The abyss or eternity
With God
Or with them
On a bed in some familiar
Or unfamiliar dwelling

Dead Woman Dancing on Her Grave

I've been hidden
In trials and tribulations
Tossed with tempest
Laden with scorn
Eaten the bread of sorrow
Drank from the cup of bitterness
Rotten to the core

I have been spewed
Out of the mouth of hatred
Regurgitated indifference
Repented of sins
I've not committed
Knowing that
Where humans walk
Sin stalks relentless
In the near or distance

I have stood in heaven
And hell
In awe of the One
And of the other
Unafraid
I've seen demons rise from the pit
To assail my soul
Then seething
Returned to the pit
Victimless

Doris Wellington

But more so
I have gazed upon what was not
To understand what hibernates in the deep

The ancestors come before the throne
Beseeching God for a voice
To vindicate those
Who have never spoken
Beyond the wall of ashen graves
Bound in anonymity
Silenced by greed of spirit
And I rise
To commit
Here am I Lord
Send me…

The Plan of Salvation
If Sister Rachael Raises Her Hand Three Times

Thirty-eight years ago
I bowed my knees on a concrete floor
At the church by the railroad tracks
A lopsided picture of Jesus
Hung behind the podium
A vague shadowy figure
Of a woman approached
And kneeled beside me
I heard David Penn fleecing God
Concerning his call to ministry
*"If Sister Rachael waves her hand
Three times
I'm a minister!"*

Yes...
I want to pray with him
Lift my voice above the worn snare
My brother James is banging
While singing off key

*If I can help some stranger find their way
Then I have done my earthly deed*

The supplicants joined him in the chorus
"Then my living will not be in vain"
And I raised my ignorant innocence
To God and cried
Until salt tears watered my longing

Save me O' Lord!
I am a sinner
Of no fault of my own
Blame Adam
But don't leave me here
On this altar of repentance
With no hope of being changed
Naked and barren

Save me O'Lord
From an alcoholic father
Dragging his demons
From generations gone by
To the center
Of our poverty-stricken existence

Save me
From the toil of cotton
And the smell of tobacco
Still branded in my flesh

Save me
From trying to help Mudd
Every time dad gets the urge
To pull that pistol from his pocket
And threaten her
For no reason at all
Except he's drunk

Save me from the memory
Of jumping between
His loaded gun
And Mudd's raised hatchet
Fed up to the brim and overflowing
From taking his crap

Save me
I'm lost without a
future
So
I skipped college
To hang around the house

I didn't trust that dad
Wouldn't do her harm
So
I took a job
At Cameron Station
And stayed there
for a while

And sure enough
During all my moaning
I looked up just in time
Sister Rachael waved her hands
Three times

And then slowly
As Sister Wilborne opened the door
Pastor Wright rolled her eyes
I counted Sister Rachael's fourth wave
Lifted to celestial skies
Against David's feverish imploring

O' Lord
Save me from doubting
Sister Rachel waved her hands four times
What do you want me to do now?

My throat is hoarse
From calling your name
My knees are knotted
From a dank November floor
My fingers are numb from clapping
My teeth rattle from speed calling
"Je- Je-Jesusssss!"
Without benefit of breathing
The louder the more believable

Dead Woman Dancing on Her Grave

Save me from tarrying
From drowning in weary
Entertaining suicidal pity

For not knowing my purpose
And for still questioning
Your existence

Save me O'Lord
Before Christmas Eve
So
I will not be
An unbelieving heathen
With nothing to celebrate

It is my cry
My endless yearning
If You are here or there
Come and prove it
Right here
Right now
In the midst of my longing
Despite my doubts
And reservations

Doris Wellington

Save me O' Lord
Lift my head
Do not leave me I pray
To return to the projects
Without salvation

And so
I remember
As clearly as any visitation since
The rush of calm that entered my spirit
The cool ginger breathing against my cheek
Like the whispering pines of a quiet night

The strength of a force
I could not see
Lifted me upward upon my feet
As new tears
Cascaded upon the floor

The world stopped around me
And I lifted my faith
As an offering unto the grace of God
"Those who call upon the Name of the Lord
Shall be saved"

Dead Woman Dancing on Her Grave

And in that moment of my serene
That church by the tracks couldn't contain
What I'd just received
In immeasurable joy

Saved
To the upmost
I believed
From the sins of Adam
And the burden of Eve
(Whatever that means)
I am saved…

Saved
From needing to understand
About that and this
Or this and that
Too far in
I can't look back

And so
I turned
To the vague
Shadowy figure of the woman
Eyes filled with tears
I hugged my mother's joy

Doris Wellington

Together we danced
Arm and arm
For she too
Had received the Lord

Thirty-eight years and counting
We still eat
From his bounty
Mom and I
Still reverently speak
Of that night we received
Jesus Christ

No more
Eli-Eli lama Sabacthani

Praise Dancing Salvation

God
You birthed me
From an embryo of silent longing
Wandering on the brink
Of expectation
But never fulfilled
Walking
To redundancy
That did not sleep
Hoping
But afraid to dream
Dreaming
But afraid to believe
Believing
Against the tide of fear
That held captive my life
That plummeted
Night after night
In the bottomless pit
Where those abandoned
Drink from the belly of the abyss
Or so I believed

Doris Wellington

Songs composed
Are consumed by the perils
Of hell
Never again to comfort

I was there
An eternity
In the uterus of the grave
No light found me
Evil imposed its will upon my desire
And I stood interposed
Between
Night and day
Deliverance and damnation
Restlessness and repose
Joy and confound despair
Hope without expectation
Wretched and bewildered
Parched and pricked
Diseased
But no cure found me
Greatness
Dwarfed
By destitution of spirit
Surrounded me
Potential rotted on the vine

Dead Woman Dancing on Her Grave

Still
I cried
And wailed inwardly
Disinherited
By misunderstanding
And spirit wearied

But determined
To find a decisive entrance
Holding on to holding on
Stepping out on anything present
Praying
Pitying my own state of lost
Lost in my own state of pity
Weeping
But not willing to die
Not yet

For I glimpsed a page
Of a certain truth
Aimed at an uncertain past
That held promise for a certain future
For God so loved the world
That He gave his only begotten Son
(Word embodied)
That whoever believes
Shall not perish
But they shall have…

Possess as reality
Embrace as tangible
Receive as substance
Touch as visible
Grasp as present
Eternal
Forever
Perpetual existence

Everlasting
Never Ending
Unceasing dominion
Continuous
Undying
Unbroken fellowship
In the presence of God

And I bowed
November 14
Thirty-five years and counting
To accept without knowledge
Without the presence
Of any reasonable facsimile
The promise of God
To make me whole

Dead Woman Dancing on Her Grave

No lightening flashed
Or thunder roared
No angels tiptoed across my decision
Not that I can remember
But what I can recall
Is quite memorable
The peace that permeated
My very existence
The grip of death would try to follow
But no access was given
As I crossed the chasm
Of the dying to the living

The loftiness of believing
Gripped my days
Could it be happening?
Was an eternity of fetters
Surrendering
Where were the fears
That had possessed my sanity
My hands
My feet
My head
My heart
What on earth had heaven begot
My name
My future
My destiny

In one act of grace
Forever forgiven
No grave
No death
No hell
No demon
No devil
No Lucifer
No satanic conspiracy
Could hold back the flood
That birth
The resolve
Of my steadfast decision
And...

Unlocked the book of my tomorrow
Erased a thousand yesterdays
From my history
And the edit of death against me
Today
I still believe
I'm still free
Still saved

The price I pay
I can't expound

Dead Woman Dancing on Her Grave

To live inside the mind of God
To be stalked by devils
Impotent of power
To abort my purpose
I am not eulogized
I am crowned
There is no pity for the valleys
No penchant for the mountain
Or the arrest of fallow
Intentions
I have no desire for the honor of men
Lest I falter from this place
Of privilege

Eyes have not seen
Ears have not heard
Neither has it been revealed
To those who hate
Without a cause

Extracting
Extravagance
From His bosom
Implanted in an earthen vessel
Named Doris
Remembering my youth

That Sabbath morn
In Wilson
When an
Amorphous
Untypical child
Stood to the call of the clarion Voice
Who shall I send
And who shall go for us

I stood
In awkward timidity
I could not then
Or now
Define

Still
I came
To the altar with strangers
Harboring the secrets of their fears
And the errors of their past

Who shall I send
And who shall go for us
Enters the faint response of a child

Dead Woman Dancing on Her Grave

Here am I
Lord…
Send me
Unwavering
In my position

They wrapped a white sheet
Around my decision
And pronounced me
A candidate
For water baptism
But it could've been
Any color
Because all have sinned
And fallen short

Baptist water
Free will and freewheeling
Not to be confused
With Pentecostal fervor
Holy Rollers
They called them
For lack of discerning

Five years later
I would stand with them

Doris Wellington

Saved
Sanctified
Holy Ghost beaming

Life filled with contradictions
But not paradoxical
What seemed ambiguous
Was reconcilable

My heart was stern
And my face made flint
For all of what
Conversion consists
Healing
Body soul and spirit

The walls of my heart
Expanded
The place of my tent enlarged
God strengthened my stake
And lengthened my cord
My capacity and patience
For people evolved
And life as I knew it
Surrendered to God

Dead Woman Dancing on Her Grave

My lips
My tongue
My ears and teeth
My heart
And mind
My hands and feet
Multiplied…
I gave me to You
A mere child
You gave me back
Multiplied

Portions plump
And full of life
More than I had to give
In return

I gave you thirteen childhood poems
You gave me back
Thirteen thousand more
I gave you inchoate ability
You gave it back
In dreams and visions
Too vast to number
To God to dismiss

Doris Wellington

I laid my plans upon the altar
You gave them back
Laden with purpose
The gift of praise
And profound wisdom
The answer to petitions
I'm yet to utter

I sacrificed the pursuit of the letter
You filled my soul
With enviable treasures
Hidden from the wise and prudent
For which they search
In futility

I stripped my earthly garment bare
You covered me with righteousness
I offered the simple prayer of faith
You gave me the world to change
Earth daughter
Of Africa born

Feet shod with holy oil
Lips anointed with hieroglyphics
Poured from my Father's Spirit

Dead Woman Dancing on Her Grave

My tongue the pen
Of a ready prophet
Unfolding mysteries
Spoken in secret

I am blood born
Adopted
I carry the seal
Of my righteous Father
My DNA incorruptible

Baptized
Into a divine covenant
I act out the power
I inherited
In the womb of God

This occasion
Commemorates strength
How far I've come
How much I've grown
Through each battle
And wind of change
I've come forth
immersed in a beauty
Defined only by faith

Doris Wellington

The Me That I Am

July 8, 2010

Today I was celebrated
A young suitor thought me beautiful
And he wrapped me in praise
Fashioned for a queen
He serenaded my womanhood
With adjectives
That made my spirit soar
Beyond the tide of clouds
I am dynamic
My life is the depth
And height of dreaming
I am never barren
Never without a moment
To celebrate the me
That has evolved
Through the simple
And unpretentious
Greatness found me

And flows profusely from my being
I pause
To celebrate the me that I am

Dead Woman Dancing on Her Grave

I paid the price to be the me that I am
I didn't get to be me at a rummage sale

I didn't win me in a bingo game
It took years to master the me that I claim

It wasn't a cheap ride from there to here
I'm still paying for the me that I am

It wasn't
The toss of a coin
A bet or a dare
That I would never reach
The me that I am
It wasn't cost effective
I didn't cut corners
The me that I am
Was all or nothing

No thrills or frills
Or midnight specials
Just bowing my life
In unconditional surrender
Trudging up the downward hill
To touch the soul
of the me that I am

Doris Wellington

Tossed and driven
Buk'd and scorn
Stalked by demons before I was born

I didn't get to me tripping and jiving
I had to choose between purpose and pleasure
The me that I am
Is an authentic treasure
No forgery
No fakes
Or pretentious humility
No depreciation
Or reduction given
No consideration
To the highest bidder

It cost me greatly
To be the me that I am
Death by conviction
Family and friends
The price was not negotiable
For the me that you envy

Dead Woman Dancing on Her Grave

Could you have borne
the cross I carry
Days on end of self-denial
Fasting and praying
Aching from hunger
The me that I am
Was birth in loneliness
The fruit of trial and tribulation

Patient in suffering
Tempered by waiting

The me that I am
Survived holding on
Resilient
Steadfast
Unmovable

The portrait you see
Is not a copy
It bears the signature
Of an appraised original
The scars are real
Etched to soul
The me that I am
Is certified GOLD
Indisputable

Doris Wellington

My Mocker's Lament

I did not know that she would rise
To such accolades in this lifetime
Or I would not have taken the lead
In naming her
Least likely to succeed
Nor withheld the gifts to help her climb
To heights I thought
She would never surmount
I did not believe that she would be
So great as to inspire
dreams in me

She gathers the spoil of every test
And holds it captive in her fist
Turns her face toward the wind and
Soars to places I've never been
And no doubt I never will
Because my courage unlike her faith
Was nothing but a mask
Compared to her
Undaunted strength

Dead Woman Dancing on Her Grave

Defying all negatives
She ascends nobly to her place
With charismatic dignity
Sharing as she always did
Bits of kindness with foe
And friend

Now within my haunted soul
Left to wonder on my own
If she has not always been
What I envied
Even then…

Doris Wellington

War Dance
November 10—4:00 AM

Do you know your strength
What you've endured to conquer
For you the dead has been raised
Graves have been left bare
You invited the contempt of hell
Angels tiptoed into the camps of your enemy
And slaughtered their PLANS
To leave you dead

Applaud your history
It's a history of purposed survival
Haphazard survival
Obstinate
Willful survival
Survival despised during
Continued existence
Persistent despite
You resist for all who sleep
And believe harder because you know
What you have to resist
To honor your gifts
Honor what divinity has bore
Honor your mother
The evidence
Of her intractable resolve

The testimonies are endless
If you want to know the definition of success
Look in the mirror
The reflection doesn't lie
You're still here
You want to know the essence of faith
Embrace yourself

Look around you
Your fruit bear witness
That you didn't quit
All around you is a victory

And behind every victory
An adversary defeated
Lurks in fear
Of your continuance
For every day you continue
Defeats an enemy
Your indomitable spirit defies the odds
And bore greatness
And how is that greatness defined
How you see yourself

Applaud your history
Poverty couldn't hold you
Death released its grip
Because you didn't stop
To acknowledge its existence
You raised a nation to believe

Wrap your arms around your spirit
Around a future still unclaimed
Claim it now
And all its possibilities
Whatever you leave the world
Leave it the legacy
Of a woman who dreams
The spirit of prevail
Buoyancy of faith
Tried in the fire of affliction
Fully surrendered
Pure gold
A thousand times
More victorious than failure
Could ever produce
Choreographed by angels
Who watch your every move
Chart your path
Around worlds
You have yet to compass
And steady your sword
of war

Do not despise where you are
No one shares your pity

No one numbers your faults
Or stands in awe of your loss
Except those who like you
Conquer in spite of

Dead Woman Dancing on Her Grave

Born to be free
Delivered to reign
Your fullest breath
Yet to be breathed
In God
Live
Move
And have your being
Your brightest hour
Is yet to shine
Your magna opus yet to seize

Covering you with grace and truth
I see your heart
There is no truce
Just another stage to replenish
Then back a watchman over the living
Your greatest dream
You're yet to fulfill
Your mustard seed
Is yet to yield

Do not abandon
The prayers you've prayed
Your most cherished harvest
Lies beyond this rain
Your victories waltz
Behind your tears

Holds covenant promises
I'm about to reveal

I hold time and eternity
In my hand
You're never too late
According to plan

Inquire of a woman
Stooped and bowed
Eighteen years hurting
And scarred

The Syro-Phoenician
And the woman at the well
Sarah at eighty-nine
And the daughters of Zelophehad
Ask Harriet Tubman
About the movement she led
Through the Underground Railroad
With fainting spells

Women who could not read nor write
Moved mountains by day
Birthed nations by night
Challenged by every conceivable
Disadvantage
Walked on water
Without the thought of surrender

Dead Woman Dancing on Her Grave

Give honor to warriors
Who bear you witness
Praise for the gift of continuance
Even when weary

You've been killed more times
Than you can recall
By every which way
Except
And almost by gun
You've been stabbed in the back
And left for dead
While the guilty stood by
Trying to resurrect
Mumbling under the breath
In some foreign language
Speaking in tongues
Calling on Jesus

Pulling every trick
And scheme
Out of the bag
Maligning your name
Judging your past
Killing you softly
With deadly lies
Nailing you to the cross
Unjustified

Doris Wellington

Calling you everything
You are not
Jealousy ranting
Hating
From the pulpit
Spat on
Stepped on
Overlooked
Denied
Pulled from the furnace
Just in time

Falsely accused
Abused
To the core of the soul
By those
Who had no power
To make you whole

Beat down
Beat up
Beat down again
But you just keep rising
From the dead

Preaching Blu Woman Bluz

Do y'all have a problem
Because you look at me
like of all my preaching years
I have not seen
I have not known
the plight of woman blues
while proclaiming my faith
praying my conviction
singing my soul's
uncompromised principles

While studying myself full
fasting myself fat
rising from dreams
phenomenon
and of unknown
origin

Still
you look at me
as if I've never
been
indecently pursued
or escaped
the threat of rape

Doris Wellington

You might as well
hear it from me
I've got human scars
running down the seam of my core
men I thought friend
despise me
for saying "No"

I have a broken front tooth
that heralds my triumph
of defending my right
to protect my virginity
had I been a little weaker
a little less inclined
I would still be mourning
vagina venting
for not being desired

Men who extolled
the virtues of God
sent coded messages
from elevated thrones
soliciting
lust filled nights
indulging
their entitlement
to deviant desires

non-discriminating
lust
NO RULES
just
lust

dripping in the pretense
that the aftermath
of unbridled
sperm
would lead to the altar
of wedded bliss
Mr. and Mrs.
This or that
Pastor and First Lady
Spit or Spat
now
first lady blues
born from
men who prey

I know what it is
to hope
and pray
only to be labeled
too sanctified

Doris Wellington

Rejected
just because
not sensual
sexy
or sinful enough
to dismantle
my priestly robe
for monsters
parading as such

And yet
I tried
God knows
I tried

I cried out to be different
If I die let me die
but do not let me
be painted
with indifference
I know I am human
and being human
I've sinned
but let me not
lie in wait
for the kiss
of dead men's scourge

Dead Woman Dancing on Her Grave

For it comes
cloaked
like righteousness
behaving
like those
seeking to repudiate
wrong while
cuddled in the arms
of desensitization

Using every excuse
to embrace
endorse
and exonerate
the flesh
for engorging
the forbidden

I have been called
cold
frigid
unloving
unkind
aloof
too saved
holier than Thou

Doris Wellington

Trying to use verbal blackmail
to seduce me
into compromise
in exchange
for sheet therapy
to cure
inhibitions

Sorry
I do not have
"No More Sheets"
stories to sell
I haven't bought a pulpit
on my back
or on my knees
at the gates of hell

You think I've never
yearned and wished
for man loving
without selling my soul
to the devil
knowing
afterwards
I would be forgiven

Dead Woman Dancing on Her Grave

Preaching
justification
for willful sins
against
redemptive grace

You think I haven't
slept hugging my tears
rebuking myself
for thinking me strong
for holding on
and not sleeping
with everything
in a cleric collar
or a Brioni tailored to tempt

Pretending love
just to have
that lover's tryst
with wolves
parading
as men of God
jocks
inflated
with arrogant
disregard
for hearts

Doris Wellington

Motives
concealed
and sometimes flaunted
behind the mask
of salvation
and homiletics
delivered
from feigned lips
dripping with guile
to ensnare silly women
into
spermicidal complicity

Until they lay
uncovered
the sacred
abandoned
to places
where demons
swoop down
to collect
debts incurred
in lascivious play
and they move on
to victim umpteenth

Dead Woman Dancing on Her Grave

I have been there
but I did not stay
I have been there
but I did not wallow
I vomited the bile
of temptation
and smeared
the victory
in the face
of Satan

There
behind enemy lines
I fought
for what
women
have the right
to decide
without force

Without the threat
of intimidation
for being
stronger
than
concupiscence

Doris Wellington

Refusing
to engage
my feminine wiles
whether
pursued
propositioned
or otherwise
I decline

There is no retirement plan
for dignity
no selling
or buying
depending
on the turn of markets
and ease
of living

I live and breathe
to sleep at night
I cannot
for the sake of pleasure
bow my soul
to temporarily
gratify
unholy rites

Dead Woman Dancing on Her Grave

Driven to heights
that plummet
within a 60-second
minute
of a choice gone
wrong
or right
and has no power
for a command
performance

Just a lingering
blood tie
or a memory
of how great
or awful
the feeling
that proselytized
and disempowered
the sacred

Doris Wellington

I decline
the journey
of venting
hashing
framing
and reframing
songs of regret

to any degree
in opaque
or transparent
narratives

This was and is
my one and only time

Letter to a White Woman

White woman!
White woman
Why are you crying
Whatever your suffering
They're not like mine
Have you ever been
Hitched to a wagon
Like a mule
Flogged and whipped
And commanded to pull
Have you ever
Had your children
Torn from your tit
And thrown into the Atlantic
From a moving ship
Your girl children
Raped
In front of your eyes
And the only prayer you had was
"Lord
Let her die"

Doris Wellington

Have you ever been called
A tar-baby wench
Or a bastard whore
Just for being Black
With no remorse
Or denied the right
to live and breathe
The same air as Whites

When did you sit my children
Upon your knee
And give them your breast
From which to feed
The nourishment of life
To satisfy hunger
To live and not die
In the hope of a tomorrow

Has your son
Ever been murdered
Because of his color
Hands raised in surrender
Or tied behind
His back
With neither legal recourse
Nor the right to appeal

Dead Woman Dancing on Her Grave

Still clinging to innocence
Died in jail
Under suspicious circumstances
Never revealed

Died
For lack of air
For breathing

Or perhaps you have
After all
You're a Woman
No less and
No more
Than I am

Doris Wellington

Something Beautiful Within
February 8, 2019

Think me not frail
or low born
to man's desires
and whims
to be bartered
battered
or branded

To tantalize
his fantasies
until delirium
consumes
and bolsters
false
returns

I am no man's
shrinking violet
that underpins
his ranting jealousy
just because

I am my own song
I sing me
divine

Dead Woman Dancing on Her Grave

Inspired from
the mind I share
with the God
I bore
wrapped in an earth shawl
nine months
incubating
in my loins
I gave birth
to the Glory of God

Like
Mary
I sing praise
for I am chosen
and favored
among women

No man
need saint me
or bless me with
golden scepters
I know who I am
I came
from the presence
of infinity
fully endowed
fully commissioned
to be who I am
no apologies

So
I sing me
without repentance
or explanation
without
the need
for sacred lyrics
that rise
and fall
but never linger

I sing myself
the girth and reach of my soul
I sing me happy
to avenge laughter
yearning to burst forward
restrained by mores
shut away
and left alone

I sing myself
wide
like the river
that spat me upon
the banks
of seamless shores

Dead Woman Dancing on Her Grave

I sing myself free
unscripted
by ancient writs
that cannot
be deciphered
or rites
shaped by laws

I sing myself
dance
feet clapping
upon asphalt clouds
tapping their song
to the applause
of angels
and the bow and curtsy
of the moon
and stars

I sing myself joyful
full of glorious splendor
that cannot be bought
or bartered
by tokens
or favors
that leave rotten
upon the vine

Doris Wellington

I sing myself overflowing
in barren places
water
in desert drought
peace
in sorrow
sadness
faith
that reaches down
where love sprouts
from seeds
planted
by hate

I sing me
born of woman
strong
steadfast
and stanchion
undaunted
by the shadows
of fear
that loom
just beyond
the horizon
or fully visible
before my eyes

Dead Woman Dancing on Her Grave

I sing with destiny
across the paths
of ancient gods
who fought
valiantly
but never tasted
the blood of death
like those
who die before
the spear is pierced
before
the race commences
or the winner
or loser
declared

I sing me
warrior
fisted
and fierce
in the furnace
of my affliction
singing
the victory
where victory songs
do not belong

Doris Wellington

I sing myself
the courage
that carried my mother
across the chasm
of life
to face death
a thousand times
summoned
a thousand times
returned
unanswered

I sing me
the daughter
of gods
who snatched the spear
of giants
and carry the flag
for all the valiant

Dead Woman Dancing on Her Grave

I sing myself
impetuous
like Eve
whose restless
wandering
courted and
conversed
with Satan's
corruptible ways

and still emerged
his captor

Fierce
like my ancestors
who sat
on thrones
kings
and queens
conversing
with the stars
and dancing
with the wind
atop
or around
the Kilimanjaro

Chanting and singing Me...
unborn

Doris Wellington

Her—Category Undeclared

Precipitation forms on my brow
threatening tears
I refuse to cry
like the yield
of the annual harvest of rain
I can neither stop
nor interfere
with its fall to the ground

To Hell with your honors
and accolades
stained with superfluous
sucking up
and vomit emitting bull

For those smitten
by the wretched
ratchet approval
of man-made
make believe
fantasies
and lies
read me
sidesways
or upside down
I'm declassified

Dead Woman Dancing on Her Grave

I don't need a Grammy to inspire my rise
or celebrate what defines
my divine right to be
I'm a novelty without an Oscar
to bind me to genres
and categories
structured to deny me
when I don't measure
up to what's
expected of me
like the Tony
the American Music
Golden Globe
or Halls of this
and that
to legitimize

Or awards for the measure
of numbers sold

Platinum
Silver
Bronze
and Gold

For I will be without accolades
the depth and height
I was born to be

Though I don't oppose
the rationing of gifts

Among millions of folk
qualified to receive
the praise of those
who offer them

And yet
without recognition bought and sold

I am
the Enigma of the divine
disqualified
and set aside
to be reconsidered
as time lapses
or reevaluated
and redefined
as to whether my talent
belong with your
wunderkind

Or given by proxy
that which a more
suitable candidate
refused to accept

Dead Woman Dancing on Her Grave

Label me
mark me
unsuitable
for moral elevation
or decline

I am what I am
declassified

Place no offerings
denied me here
upon my grave
posthumously

For I've crouched in doorways
watching and waiting the day
when the world realizes
it will never know
enough of me to praise

So

leave me alone
to celebrate rejection
of orthodox inclusion

Among those neglected

No Less Fierce—

No less a Warrior

What!

Doris Wellington

You mean I'm not a woman
Just because

Some social
psychoanalyst
master of
psychological
therapy

wrote the book
on what makes a woman
who can or cannot
be classified as such
because of what?

On a scale from one and up
depending on
the most crap she took
or swallowed down
or spat up

Fighting her corner
living her truth and lies

Of this and that

Decided by whom

Am I less a woman
Just because
I haven't saved the tags and labels
of my worst experiences

Dead Woman Dancing on Her Grave

To be appraised
by those who make the rules
for survival

Or determines
what categorizes

Authentic
Womanhood

Strong
unwavering
standing tall
with her compatriots
or male counterpart

Shucks!

The research sucks
I'm a statistic
that hasn't been considered
I fell through cracks
surviving living

Refer to File Z
Last Exhibit
I was an influencer
before that hashtag
was trending

Doris Wellington

I am not a victim of circumstance
not a victor by accident
I wasn't randomly selected to survive
I am a Warrior!!!!
I fight my corner every day I rise

What must I do to be heard
who must I do to be seen
what trick must I pull
what game
what scheme
to be applauded
or paraded

What must I do
to be saved!

Is not my story
as triumphant
my survival as notable?

I am not
a watering hole for every
Tom
Dick
and Harry

Not a reality show
celebrity
SELLING my goods

To the highest bidder

Dead Woman Dancing on Her Grave

I am not a porn star
I wasn't molested as a child
by some sinister predator

I don't do weed
speed
Crack
Meth or Heroin

No
I haven't been raped
once
not EVER

Or held captive
in a bomb shelter
by a rapist
birthing his children
to call him
daddy
and grandfather "Monster"

Doris Wellington

But you weren't there
while still a teen

I fought like hell
to prevent it
one tooth still broken
helps me remember it

Am I no less a woman
because I preferred
to protect my virginity
for fighting a ravenous beast
between snorts
and threats

You're going to have my baby

While I retorted
through tears
If ever I will
but not tonight
not as long as I live

Dead Woman Dancing on Her Grave

I left his manhood
battered and wounded
he left my womanhood
intact
proving
I'm no more or less
a woman
because
I'm not doing
ten to life
for killing him
as I should've

Do I have to have
questionable baby daddies
rising from welfare
to a renowned profession
on TikTok

suspicions exonerated

on Paternity Court

or Maury Povich

Doris Wellington

Isn't my story
worth the life I've lived

Just trying to be a decent human being

No
I'm not an Ex-drug queen
selling my children
or whoring around
on my husband's
goodness
then killed him
claiming
"Battered Woman's Syndrome"
When I know full well
It was for the insurance

I didn't climb the corporate ladder
sleeping with different partners
or doing that one or this one
to get to the top

selling the dignity of womanhood
for a frontpage byline
or a reality series

Dead Woman Dancing on Her Grave

I wasn't abducted
caged and survived
but the abyss I lived
was never publicized

or sold to the Enquirer
just because
we must have our noses broken

or worse
to be considered survivals
who escaped the abuse
of domestic tyranny

or the lies we tell
to the status quo
just so
there will be no
questioning

our narratives

That we are the fittest
of the weaker and
the strongest
among women

Doris Wellington

I don't have
sex tapes to sell
no little black book
to blackmail clients

No hidden schemes

To make me a millionaire

Or authenticate
my claim of being
too tough to crack

You might as well
hear it from me
I've got regrets
running down the seam
of my soul
men I thought friends
despise me
for saying "No"

Dead Woman Dancing on Her Grave

But
I'm not doing time
for killing my baby's daddy
or the husband
I caught
with the gardener
the nanny

Or the boy next door
in a crime of passion
punishable
in the court of law
for a premeditated
act
committed
in the heat of the moment

Really…

Now in prison
I preach the gospel of Jesus
while writing my memoirs
for killing my children

Doris Wellington

negotiating
a spot
on primetime streaming
to tell my version
of being wrongfully
convicted
when I know
I was inappropriate
with my student
speaking of course
of those who are

Do I have to be a perfect specimen
the goddess every man
seeks to please him
the first selected
the last one to know
that he was a pervert
in sheep's clothing

Am I no less to be celebrated
because I outed the hypocrisy
of men and women

Who live the lies
of preachers and mentors
while all the time
behind closed doors
they seduce
and disrobe innocence

Dead Woman Dancing on Her Grave

Must I
be a villain
just because
my story is not
encased in drama

That spills across
every time zone
exposing my demons
just because
it's fashionable

Is there no dignity
in keeping close to the heart
my own sins and iniquities
by keeping silent
and bearing my own burdens
in the heat of the storm
without a crowd to applaud
my stubborn resolve
as if it's expected
for everyone to fall

Can I get some love
because I resisted
the temptation
to post
on social media
my every triumph
as a photo op

Doris Wellington

Let me be clear
this one moment
on paper
will be the first and
last time I will proclaim

I am a survival
among the fittest
in body
mind and spirit

And for the record
the preponderance

of the evidence
supports the narrative
that follows from this point

Born in the grasp of
malignant poverty
to uneducated
migrant
poor
sharecroppers
working tobacco
for clothes and school supplies
that never came
first things first
rent and utilities

Dead Woman Dancing on Her Grave

There is no debating it
I should not have survived

from such a template
as my parentage

but my mother
didn't pimp me
or prostitute for survival

She worked long days
in domestic
and nights in a factory
separating dried tobacco

So

by example

I didn't sell
my body for vices
or abandon my children
for some no count
primate
masquerading
as a man

Doris Wellington

She wasn't ignorant
or unlearned
just without the education
to pass on
what the refinements of breeding
affords

But give me some credit
for the dignity
of a mother
who despite disadvantages
raised eleven children
with the strength
of formidable

She taught me by example
to take pride in who I am

You don't have to wallow with dogs
to be accepted by the pack

You don't have to lie
cheat
or steal
to gain in life
what perishes with the years

Dead Woman Dancing on Her Grave

Hold up your head
be proud
of what you have
your greatest story
is the one you live

Your greatest asset
is not your booty
your breast
or your body

But the head on your shoulder
and what's inside of it

Never expect
that the world owes you anything
it's your responsibility
to choose how you're
be remembered

While others are fighting
to make a name for themselves
by whatever means
at the price
of whomever

Doris Wellington

Must I be a sex symbol
or bombshell
to be remembered

Or a naked
centerfold
to be desirable
or sensual

No

I don't have one baby daddy
I've never bore a child
never miscarried

But I've been stalked
harassed
and weeks abandoned

by a bisexual husband
who stole my identity
left me for trash
to be swept away like litter
in putrid garbage bags
mistreated just because
my genitalia identity
was not
the same as his

Dead Woman Dancing on Her Grave

And yet
he courted me
and made promises
"to death do us part"
all the while
committing
the ultimate fraud

Abusing the authority of the state
entering into an agreement
he had no intentions
of keeping
stealing and robbing
lying and cheating
turning a good dream
into a nightmare
hemorrhaging

Blood strewn
across nations
like menstrual

That seeped
through the veins
of history
without witnesses
until the universe
demanded payment and
he was slain still spewing bile

Doris Wellington

No

I wasn't sold into sex slavery
kidnapped for a drug lord
molested by father
or a mother
of equal sinister behavior

But I prayed
God knows I prayed
and labored feverishly
sometimes without sleep
months of days

Fasting without food
beseeching
knocking on doors
in letter campaigns
and calls
to intervene
for children who
cannot sleep
because
some sorry excuse
of a human being
won't let them

Dead Woman Dancing on Her Grave

Trolling the streets
and school yards
playgrounds

and college dorms

watching doggishly

through cracked windows
and opened blinds
seething with lustful eyes
masturbating
secreting
semen upon the grounds

Hell to the No!
I might not get a photo shoot
or a front page
alongside a celebrity name

Or an online
interview
with Who's Who
among the famed

But I stood up
went all the way
to Capitol Hill
pleading for answers

Doris Wellington

I Called
religious leaders
on the carpet

Yelled and screamed
intolerance
for
high crimes
and sins
against children
behind the veil of my grief
no bells
toll for me
no doors swing on welcome hinges
no VIP access
or keys to the city

No prime time special
or Emmy
no walk on the red carpet
for the best documentary
I'm like millions
of unsung WOMEN
who survive and
succeed to tell it

Walking and wailing
like Rachel
for her children
no songs
no requiem

no interview with Oprah
no chart stopping
listing
on American Billboard

Just being present
rising
and dressing
everyday
walking the valley
of the shadow of death
fearing all evil
because you care
duped
disrespected
denied
disconnected
no sheet stories
worth mentioning
no airing of garbage
to turn friends
into followers

Doris Wellington

No calling The Star
or spilling the beans
on anyone
I can only do my
best

I will not deconstruct me
and I will not be confined
to the one size fits all
template designed
for women who resist being cloned

Who are you
to tell me
how to shape my story
how to live it
or how I saw it
just because
it doesn't conform
to the conventional format
spun by those
clueless to my backstory

Dead Woman Dancing on Her Grave

Dr. This
Professor That

Bystanders
spectators
and professional critics

Don't get it twisted
I applaud women of fortitude
who triumph
amid
all the crap
we endure as women
inequities
stereotypes
titles of obscenities
indecent proposals
or attempts
to destroy
dismantle
our progress
or
altogether
disenfranchise
or discredit
our will to continue

Doris Wellington

Bravo!
Bravo!
a thousand times
to a thousand drumbeats
and fiddlers

But don't lump us under one banner
though some are universal
others are varied
accordingly
to this or that
the when and where
and the what of whom

Of the who I am

Undeclared

Dead Woman Dancing on Her Grave

First I Am

June 28, 2020

I am bred
bridled
face exposed
behind veiled
illiteracy
education
prohibited
or used
against me
vile
conspiracies
to contain me
constrain me
suppress
my intelligence
rename me

children
snatched
from the womb
of the future
by the bastard hands
of abusers

Doris Wellington

Covered
in rusty cans
that move garbage
and dumped
into land fields
never discovered

DNA exhumed
but never liberated
perpetrator
exonerated
case closed
for generations

My seed silenced
by Epitaphs
in numbers

But there are no awards
given for being absent
by no fault of your own

Who will raise my children
or how will they remember
what they never knew
the fragrance of my being
the lullaby whispers
upon their cheeks
or the sound of my voice
summoning them

Dead Woman Dancing on Her Grave

I've been threatened by the best
instructed to
Cease and Desist
or else

Bend to our religious principles
bow or we will break the door
of your defense
we seek to coop your strength
suck the inner core of your spirit
until it's drained of selfness

And there is nothing
left of you
familiar
then we can
pour into you
clone you
in the name of God
make and
mold
and shape you
into whatever
has no identity
in itself
because now
you fit
into the society
born of blood rites

Doris Wellington

Religions
and establishments
that demand
you be
anything
other than yourself

Look at them
imprisoned
by the doctrines
of man
devoid of healing

Ensnaring
those
already captive
into the net
of the half-witted

So Do Your Best

Episodic Update: Do Not Post
9-16-2017

Whiskey drips from an uncorked bottle
my inside yields to the whispers
of liquor dreams
that will not let me rest
the clacking of stilettos
and rustling satin
swish across the brain
drunken stammering lips
spew dead fermented words
against the slumbering night air
with no certain direction
arrows from an aimless bow
search for me
but I am not there
so leave me alone in this dark
eating and drinking
from the banquet
of the dispossessed
no tomorrow awaits me
neither tears nor jovial laughter
arouse the sobering
for there will be none
not tonight
not for many nights hence

Doris Wellington

No fortnight
nor Sabbath
there will be no rain
to quench my dry parched hope
begging only to taste
what makes for merriment of soul
but there will be no dancing
no celebratory song
just inebriated soliloquies
and no one to answer
the rant and rancor of madness
that has drawn boundaries around the heart
I am beyond amusement
beyond dancing with shadows
I prefer to wallow in the bile
that spews its stench
upon other folk joy

To conceal layers of decayed pain
pain that has morphed into debauchery
on steroids
Do not dance for me
with me or
because of me
do not dance in view of my gaze

Dead Woman Dancing on Her Grave

I am beyond amusement
beyond reveling without a cause
I prefer to wallow in the bile
that spews its stench
upon other folk dreams

I am lost
do not cry for me
your lamentations
will uselessly invite
my contempt
for I have no more tears to cry
for me
not even love can excavate
from swelling tides of self-deprecating
chagrin

Leave me alone
I have not called for thee
I have not mourned above a whisper
that suffocates on contact
with the lifeless loathing
bequeathed me
children I never bore
have died in the womb
and those I birth
are scattered to places unknown
seeking refuge

Doris Wellington

I cannot give
what sorrow I could not absorb
in profligacy
I have tried in futility
to sop up in pills and bottles
that lie empty upon shelves
with labels
that bear names for conditions
designed for me
that not even I can pronounce
or renounce

my husband has turned
to those more suited for living
I have drained him
of his pity
and he has no more for me
he has been inoculated
from what ails me
he seeks asylum
among the caring
which I am neither

Dead Woman Dancing on Her Grave

Buried beneath dubious
and faithless dreaming
I have hidden myself
from the prying eyes of strangers
and neighbors who look
but cannot see my despair
nor hear the rift of water
that flows from a life broken
beyond repair
or the blood that screams
down my arm
or the stone that presses
relentless
upon my chest

I seek neither understanding
nor pity
intervention
nor
empathy
only to be left alone
only to be left alone

Alone
I tell you
Leave me
 A……………………………….LONE…………………

Doris Wellington

I scream life
but you turn a deaf ear
to answer your indifference
I romp naked
but you turn your gaze to flowers
along the river's edge
where I contemplate
death

Vexed to neglect
infected
rejected
by troubles
uncontested
by the restless
waging
burdens
I bear

Dead Woman Dancing on Her Grave

I am a prisoner
held captive
not by fear
for I do not fear
I cheer
hold dear
revere
let nothing outside of me
interfere
with my tears

So
leave me I pray
to the wiles of myself
I roam in and out
back and forth
hither and thither
between two worlds
that console my ambiguity
and I am never disappointed
by what they give
for they expect nothing of me
but to yield
to the invigorating light
of ignorance
that engulfs my indecisions

Doris Wellington

Or my right
to be left alone
those as hapless as I
paint themselves
holier than Thou
self-righteous snots
who have no certain direction
or they wouldn't be so inclined
to meddle in my world
where all that matters
is that I am happy
in whatever state
I find myself

I rejoice in my sorrow
I'm patient in tribulation
when I am without hope
I'm never without an anchor
appearances aside
I gather strength
from the masters
to conquer
I must surrender
to surrender
I must conquer
to move forward
I retreat

Dead Woman Dancing on Her Grave

Or sometimes stand still
to gain new momentum

You might think me strange
compressed inwardly
by improbabilities
that narrow my perception
inscrutable
but I am neither
yet both
simultaneously
existing alongside of the other
negotiating
what
when
how
and why?
hoping against hopelessness
afraid to hope
lest my thoughts are discerned
for thinking I too can be helped
I pray and fast
for what or whom I don't know
and most likely
I do not care
but probability aside

Doris Wellington

I reach beyond the broken places
where my petitions
are dried stained watermarks
that form unusual reminders
that I have been here before
and I am lost again
until found

until someone more tolerable of me
than I am of myself
whose faith in God
is stronger than my strongest nightmare
whatever that is
and whose shoulders
gravity does not affect
when I am near

speculating without probable leads
probing without microscopic depth
that penetrates
beneath eye level
the porous surface
of dead skin and
pathogenic matter
unfathomable
decaying
to putrefied stench

Dead Woman Dancing on Her Grave

Buying time
until I am found

and as certain as I am lost
whenever and wherever

that realization
reincarnates
reverberates
in real time brain response
or is not trapped
between left and right
crossing
the longitudinal fissure
or a red-light signal
that momentarily pauses thought
I am certain
I will be found

I always am
always caught before ensnared
by the illusion of a perfect sanity
that robs the self
of what is inglorious
in pursuit of what is more
gloriously accepted
as normal

Doris Wellington

Stifling
constrictive
profoundly
prohibitive

by those who control
the education of the mind

Forbidding the trespassing
of madness
upon pristine grounds
sanitized by clinicians
rather than the narratives
of experience
stories that need no corroboration
or evidence to the contrary
cannot be contradicted
because
I have lived it
line upon line
precept upon precept
in theory
and practice
book
verse
And line

Dead Woman Dancing on Her Grave

Lived it
every way it could be lived
metaphoric
and literal
iambic
and pentameter
sonnet
and ballad
until the mind secretes
and hemorrhages
sanity
bruised and broken
by minds in need of fixing
forcing a square peg into a round mold
and vice versa
relentlessly
determined
for the sake of science
and complicity
reasoning that obscures identity
bashing heads against
institutionalized directives
when all I SEEK
is freedom

Free verse and
free style
without construct or measure
without judgmental labels
or social or scientific experiments
that uses
then discards
until I am found
in a lab
compared to rats
and mice
poked and prodded until useless
for anything
except notes for a lecture
to teach the inquisitive
how to avoid the inevitable
pitfalls of the delusional
forced off the road
by detachment disorders
and psychosis
that polarize
to rage
medicate to zombie
and thrown to the lions
to fight without a weapon
strong enough to win

Daily regimens
relegated to pill swallowing
as substitute for living
and designer labels
and abbreviations
for public tampering
or protest ranting

hypo this
pre that
post something or another
psychosomatic
syndromes
disorders
phobias
and challenges
AD
BD
ADHD
ED
MD
OCDD

ODD
PDD
SED
and MORE

Doris Wellington

Always MORE
Mostly Overstated Rational Education
never LESS
Less Engaging of Spiritual Structure
where it all breaks down
unless you find some order there
hence this tirade
this rambling
of how
I once was lost

once blind
but now I see
an underscored
delusion
~~strike through~~
<mark>highlighted</mark> and all
labeled
and intrusive

Dead Woman Dancing on Her Grave

Amplified[12]
mortified
tossed
scattered to the wind
presupposing
what they didn't know
was in that moment
hidden

The twists and turns
that have no hands
at least
none that are visible
thrust themselves into the loins of fate
to snatch me upward thither

I once was lost
but now I'm found
still blind
but now I see
life doesn't come in bundles
that we can choose on sight
fraught with all its troubled spots
unexpectedly

Doris Wellington

I live to conquer
moment by moment
rather than
some distant future
unpredictable
neatly packaged
and achieved

For therapeutic
cleansing

every battle I enter today
in body
mind
or spirit
war is waged
with or without my consent
to win or lose it
thus
whether lost or found
I choose to fight in
No
Other
World
than NOW

Do Not Dance
Until I Am Found

I am not yet found
I sit upon a heap of invisible garbage

Upon my gravestone
looking down
witnesses
without eyes
pass me along
without knowledge
of my existence
I scream
but ears are deaf to my cry

One day
I will be washed ashore
In the meantime

I refuse to die
In anonymity
the universe is now
my voice
in forensic science
and truth
unearthed
in land fields
of putrefied remains

Doris Wellington

Or overgrown
dumping sites

along highways
and mine shafts
or bottomless
wells

Under a slab
of concrete
in the backyard
or bound
to weights
and cast from moving
boats
or aircrafts

most likely

decapitated
and
dismembered

refrigerated

or stored

in suitcases

for easy transport

Dead Woman Dancing on Her Grave

Leaving
trace evidence
along paths

thought cleansed
and deodorized

with ammonia
and incense
still

I am not dead
there is no grave
that can hold
my body
no chains
to bind my spirit

You scatter my bones
across miles
of spacious
geographical terrain

But one strand of hair
one drop of moisture
one lone print
from thumb
or palm

Doris Wellington

One distinctive
bite mark
or button

one slither
of saliva
or sperm

one sleepless
watchful
neighbor

one prior conviction
forgotten
will find you

Years may slip
detectives
will die
and cases go cold
and revived
by more thorough
searching
a more determined
resolve
new advances
in technology

Dead Woman Dancing on Her Grave

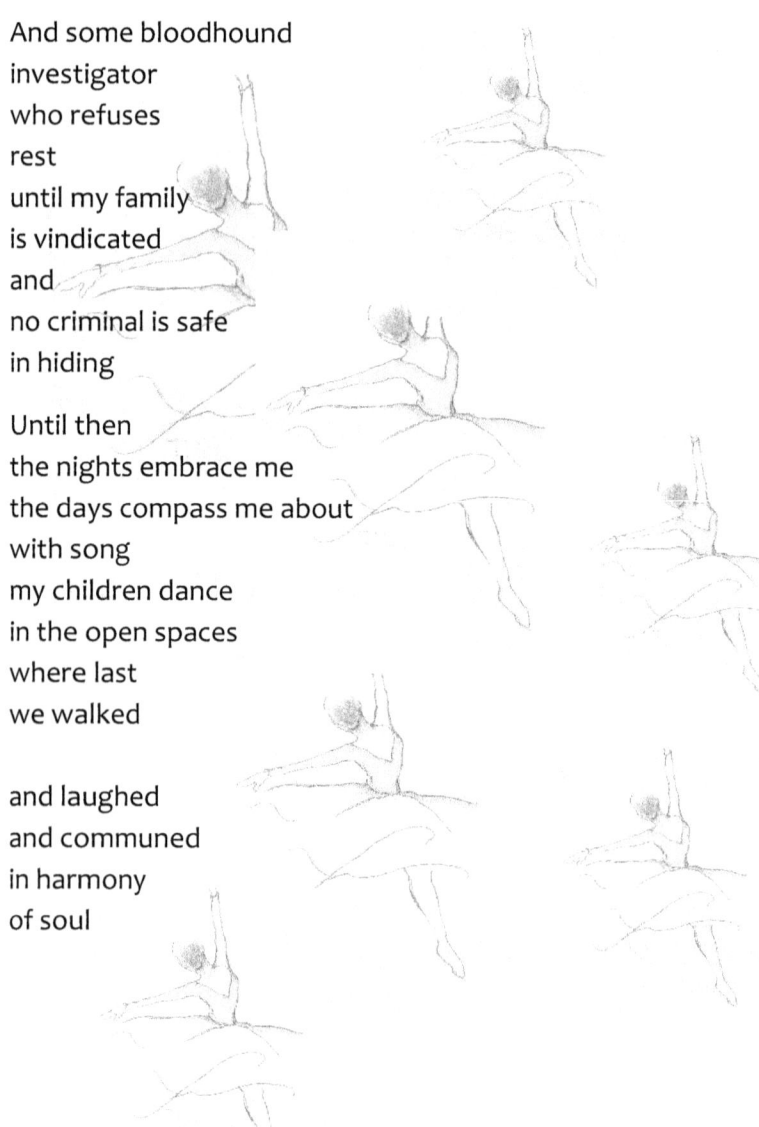

And some bloodhound
investigator
who refuses
rest
until my family
is vindicated
and
no criminal is safe
in hiding

Until then
the nights embrace me
the days compass me about
with song
my children dance
in the open spaces
where last
we walked

and laughed
and communed
in harmony
of soul

Doris Wellington

If I should ever cry
it is for those
who think me dead
that their hatred
killed me
upended my times

In human form

I watch them
through portals
parallel to theirs
never suspecting
that I'm there
to insure
that they never sleep
for sins
they commit
without remorse

I am the avenger
of those
who cannot
avenge themselves
quietly
I wait

Dead Woman Dancing on Her Grave

To recompense
the wicked
who live among
the unsuspecting
In veiled evil

heaven will send its rain
ten thousand years
but the sins against me
cannot be purged
my blood trickles

to the core of
the earth

fossilized remains

commingling
in rituals
with the innocent
slain just because
predators lurk

we have become
one voice
with the universe
heralding one message

Doris Wellington

Earth has no children
that it cannot
identify
in blood and bones
one thousand millenniums
left to decompose

I am not yet found
but I am present
In forensic thought
and when time finds me
hidden
among
dead things
thought lost
With the passing of eyes

Do not applaud
until I am found
then dance with me
on the ruins
of my ashen remains
set my epitaph in stone
I once was lost
but now I'm found
dancing on my grave

I Waltzed with God the Morning of Genesis
Excerpt

Somewhere between
the abyss and eternity
where heaven and earth
once coexisted
before chaos
in Meridian Provenance

I waltzed with God
the morning of Genesis
felt the pulse
of the universe
the heartbeat
of humanity

When Sovereignty
travailed
giving birth
to divinity
my eyes witnessed
the Big Bang Theory

Doris Wellington

As nature unfurled
in her pageantry of splendor
festooned
embellished
in colorific wonder

Stretching
and shaping
boundaries and borders
across vast terrain
and unchartered waters

Africa
Asia
Australia
Europe
India
North and
South America

I waltzed with God
from an exalted villa
of the perpetual

Dead Woman Dancing on Her Grave

As billions
of galaxies
separated by infinity
ejected
themselves
from the mind
of Preeminence
uniting space
and time

a phenomenon
phenomenally
different

I communed
with the Ancient
in the archives
of the Spirit
I danced with angels
the morning of Genesis

Doris Wellington

Where
every nation
color
creed
and tongue

Existed
one people
indivisible

Indigenous
and
Diaspora
In the womb of God

Integrated
related
undeniably
ONE

Dead Woman Dancing on Her Grave

Then
I waltzed
with God
in the eye
of the placenta
to Handel's Messiah
the morning of Genesis

As genius
gushed
from the epicenter
of power
on a labyrinth pursuit
of souls to endow

Penetrating
impregnating
for acts of valor
thought
impossible

I danced in the spirit
with women who vowed
to leave the world
better than was found

Doris Wellington

Mastering what men
thought theirs to conquer
commanding armies
leading scholars

Peacekeepers
Politicians
Philosophers
Poets
Pathfinders
Partisans
Patriot warriors

Scientists
Strategists
Inventors of trade
holding nations captive
in their sway

I might not dance in
earthen form
still
beyond this place
I waltz with God

Where I Dare Enter

January 12, 2010

Stalked by untitled manuscripts
That weave their stories
Into the fabric of my dreams
I do
And shall forever reverence
The prophetic hand
That guides my night
To unveil a world
Where the ordinary shrinks
Behind the mask
Of fear and trembling
And I am given
Ancient scrolls
To decipher

Where the future of others
Lay bare
As tales untold
In signs and symbols
Silhouetted against shadowy figures
Naked and
Exposed to scrutiny

Of eyes that penetrate the dark
And fill the vortex
With encrypted narratives

Testifying
To your gifts
In dreams and visions

That light that leads
I follow
To the mountain
Of inscrutable knowledge
Buried beneath
Fading hieroglyphics
Etched in stone
Revealing the unknown
In patterns
Deciphered

Dead Woman Dancing on Her Grave

Heaven and hell
Angels and demons
The seamless cord
Of past and future

The endless path
Between heaven and earth
And the abyss
betwixt and beyond the unveiling
That renders my memory
impenetrable

And I'm not certain
Of where I am
Whether here or there
Or there or here
Living or suspended
On the pallet of the cerebrum

Doris Wellington

The perpendicular aligns
With the horizontal
The vertical and diagonal
Converge
Upon the cirque of eternity
Where I stand in awe of God

Foreshadowing
Fulfilling and
Holding counsel
Upon graves
Where dead folk gather

My Decree of I Amness

I refuse to walk on the fringes of my own identity
If I question every everyday
Who I am or
What I am
Then I am not

If I accept the labels of others
despite how faulty their perceptions
Then I am

So I rise or fall
with the me that I am
whether embraced
or rejected
I am who I am

Doris Wellington

Woman

She gave birth to those who sought her demise
Cradled the hands that held her down
Washed the feet that trampled her dreams
Serenaded the ears that turned deaf her pleas
She wiped the eyes that saw her not
Kissed the lips that cursed her lot
Enlightened the mind that devised her fall
Returned with love her enemy's gall
She nurtured the vision that locked her out
Built her country without any clout
Yet from the ashes of her remains
She rises again and again
Dancing on her grave

Dead Woman Dancing on Her Grave

HER

Dedicated to My Mother's Earth Reign
May 19, 1931-Febrruary27, 2016

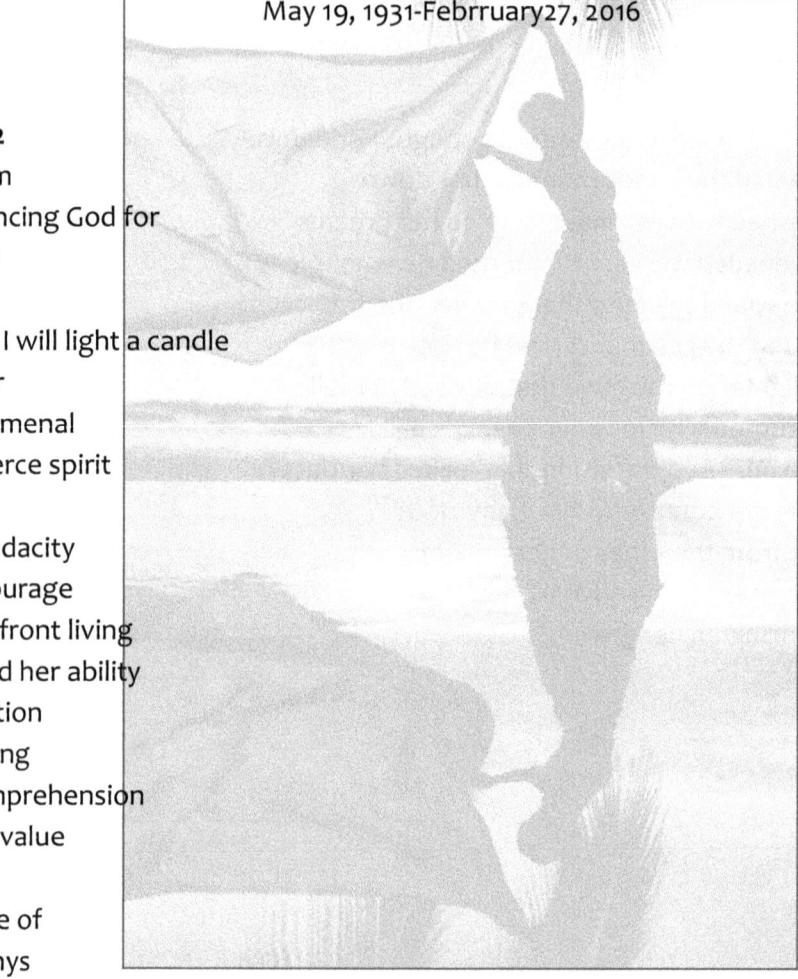

2/27/22
5:06am
Romancing God for
H. E. R

Today I will light a candle
for her
phenomenal
and fierce spirit

Her audacity
and courage
to confront living
beyond her ability
education
breeding
or comprehension
of her value

In spite of
the whys
that went unanswered
the problems
she never got to solve

But that
didn't stop her
as she moved
through phases of
uncertainty
refusing
to quit

I will hold a vigil
for her organic smile
her contagious laughter
that last gaze
into her
enigmatic presence

That forever moment
of knowing
she was passing
through the biosphere
and the valleys of Rephaim
and Anak
to the resting place
of angels and gods
tiptoeing upon
silk clouds of splendor

I will sing a favorite song
from her hymnal of many
recite her favorite poem
 "If"
by Rudyard Kipling

Dead Woman Dancing on Her Grave

I will read her favorite scripture
Isaiah 54:13
but I will never be resigned
that she's not here

I will caress her journal
of prayers
daily beseeching God
on my behalf
writing me into her heart
like loving mothers do

I will commemorate her
by continuing in faith
bearing my burdens
in the heat
of intense difficulties
and
extraordinary trials

I will summon
her formidable
her victorious
her Incredible
her "bigger than life" ideology

You must be bigger
than your pain
bigger than your afflictions
bigger than lies
and malignant bigotry

Doris Wellington

Bigger than divorce
and loss
bigger than poverty
and mistakes
bigger than the
temptation
to quit
to leave behind
unspent potential
and your dreams
in heaps

bigger than life and
the side effects
of everyday living

bigger than
domestic abuse
hunger pangs
and affection-starved
in lieu of husband love

bigger than
can't
tired
fatigue
or battle scars

Dead Woman Dancing on Her Grave

Bigger than
the abandonment of sons
who put on pedestals
jealous wives
and their insecurities

I will celebrate
her War Dance
upon the altar
her spirited
one woman performance
up and down the choir loft
her baritone
lifted to the rafters
joined by a pipe organ
and stopping feet
at Piney Grove
Freewill Baptist

"Sing, Ms. Hattie"
"Sing, Sister Wellington...
echoed parishioners
or the alto section
and she obliged

A poor humble traveler
on earth I stand alone
my faith lies
in the blood of the Lamb
Wonderful
Counselor

Jesus
my savior came
with a heart full of love
to save me from drowning
and cast off my heavy burden

The chorus burst with
adulations
she brought tears to eyes
and brightened faces
In thunderous ovation

She did not speak of poverty's lack
or penury
and doing without
she did not raise a complaint
against bland black-eyes
or powdered
government eggs

Instead she lifted
a grateful heart
Dear Lord
make us grateful hearts
for the provision
of your bounty
for the nourishment
of bodies
for Christ sakes
Amen

Dead Woman Dancing on Her Grave

Then just in case
there wasn't enough
she rubbed her hands
across her midriff
I'm just about full
I'm watching my figure

I raise my glass to toast
her conviction
never allow poverty
to inhabit the spirit
never allow it to infest
the mind
to bar you from dreaming
of a better life

Yes..
He's pleading my case
Jesus...Jesus
Wonderful Counselor

Whatever color
he's pleading
whatever the doctrine
he's pleading
real or imagined
He's pleading
whether fiction or fantasy
my faith has made
God a living reality

In me God lives
and possesses being
and by whatever other names
he indwells
Jesus… Jesus
Wonderful Counselor
my faith
has made God real

I salute
Her bowed sacred
submission
unfazed by
whispering and criticism
only 36
and already she has
eleven children
um hum…
eleven
seven girls
and four boys

Shaking hands with
impostors
behind the mask of respectability
cloaked in hypocritical
Christianity
and false Humility

Dead Woman Dancing on Her Grave

Her lips upturned
in agony praise
looking right through
their deceit
declared in their hearing
unapologetically
I'm having these children
for God

And so was her conviction
Her unwavering
unconditional
Indiscriminate
love
for them
proved it

Whether a burlap sack
across her shoulder
or her right foot propped
on a looping horse
whether cooking
ironing
or sewing on buttons
no one could rival
her laborious
no one more uplifting
or encouraging
marketing
her brand
of Bible wisdom

Doris Wellington

He that walks
with the wise will be wise
but a company of fools
will be destroyed
Honor your father and mother
that you might live long
this is the first
commandment
with promise

I seek to emulate
her
Diversity
Equity
and Inclusion
her embracing of all kinds
her love for humanity

Indigenous
diaspora
and the Native American
warrior blood
she claimed
so adamantly
her fierce
high cheek bone
toned
and sculptured

Dead Woman Dancing on Her Grave

Like her
Mother
Africa

Her
dignity
and pride
in being woman
faithfully
committed
to her husband

Driven
passionate
for family and
friends
mother
of children
she didn't birth

Her
bold
unflinching
brazen truth
in modulation
and modesty

Her audacious
panache
unrepentant

Doris Wellington

Her
snazzy
jazzy
long legs posed
statuesque
fashion model poise
edgy
inborn couturier

Her walk into a room
head turning
stares

Hey there
Ms. Hattie
you wearing
that black
patent leather belt
and matching heels

That pencil skirt
accessorizing
that white
standup collared
shirt

Dead Woman Dancing on Her Grave

Lady, you know
you looking good
in that wide brim
upside down
cup and saucer hat
that leaves spectators
gasping
trying to guess
how you keep
so fashionably
trim

She must be starving
herself to death
Luke
better watch out!
snicker...
snicker...
silent whispers

Her wife honor
intact
when Mr. Wade
pulled out a wad of fifties
but he could not tempt
her integrity
she told him where
he could stash it

So I Praise
Her
Exemplar
Teacher
by precept and example
It might not root in all of them
still she introduced them all
to her God

Her respect for education
and upward mobility
her nobility of grace
endowed
by her Maker
with hinds feet
and resilient resolve
she ran through troops
to leaped over walls

Waiting to overtake
and bind her
to mediocrity

Her late
entrance into
the halls of Academia
with a 9th grade
education and a GED
Certificate

Dead Woman Dancing on Her Grave

Shaking hands
with heads of institutions

President's
Provosts
PhDs

Her death defying
death defeating
I beat the devil running
testimony
and I'm glad

Yes you did
bruise his head
though imperfect
as we all are
stumbling
bumbling
falling short
she still remains
my earthborn
Conqueror
I pause today
to remember

H.E.R.
stubborn
fight to live
unafraid

Doris Wellington

A thousand times
stalked
and summoned
by death
a thousand times
refusing to succumb

I will die
when
and only when
I am done
and so
it was
her last will and testimony

Declare Your New Beginning

Lift your heart to God and agree with me as I declare this New Beginning over your life.

You have been transformed by and infused with divine power to subdue the earth and to have dominion. Whether you are apostle, prophet, pastor, evangelist, teacher, bishop, elder, or layman, it is not too late to walk out of the shadows of mediocrity and mere Christianity into the power and purpose that transform lives. Even your wounds can become weapons of profound healing instead of safety nets to hide your pain, mistakes, and your past.

I make this apostolic and prophetic decree over your life, your family, and everything that is *rightfully* yours. This is your day for a divine reversal of life choices gone wrong.

Rise. It's not over for you. Jesus Christ has already won the battle for your deliverance and your victory over every circumstance and condition. There is nothing to do but to rise from the ashes of self-pity and move to the mountain of praise. There is still vast, untapped potential in your loins—still mighty miracles to release—still lives to transform. It doesn't matter how long you've wallowed in regret—how repugnant the sin, Christ has provided the escape. He'll forgive you and empower your rise.

Rise. The nations slumber because you sleep—without your faith, the world lurches in darkness—creation travails to see you take your rightful place with the heirs of the universe. The Holy Spirit is waiting to pour new wine over your repentance and anoint you with a new beginning.

Rise. There's a powerful word prophesying into your life right now—to renew your strength and to crystallize your directions. How long will you lament and repent of your life; go back to the altar and reclaim your gift; go back to the willows and reclaim your song, for the future that you're entering is far greater than the past that you mourn. There is no comparison.

Rise and walk. Rise and conquer—this is your birthright! This is the mystery and the magnificence of the grace of God through Christ Jesus toward those who believe... RISE!

Doris Wellington

Former American University student and North Carolina native; Doris Wellington, is an ordained minister, spiritual life strategist, public speaker, dream analyst, and visionary writer.

Doris Wellington has effectively interwoven and branded a wide range of products, services and innovative ideas that bridge the power and potential of spirit, soul, and body. "Without this triumphant interaction, we would never understand nor could we ever apply the full range of our God-given abilities." Recognizing that the grace of our gifts comes from God, **Doris Wellington** delivers life changing spiritual, motivational, and educational conferences, media, theatre, and visionary business concepts and creative ideas.

She has authored, twenty epic stage plays, including the celebrated allegorical production, *I Waltzed with God the Morning of Genesis: A Mosaic for Peace, Dead Woman Dancing on Her Grave,* and *God, I'm Here and I'm Colored: the National Debate on Race and Equality.* She is the author of the thirteen-book poetic epistolary, *Romancing God: The Divine Love Affair*; as well as Romancing God: Memoirs of a Worshipper.

Additionally, she has authored four novels, and one memoir, *The River God Runs through Her.* She coauthored, *Stokestown: Dreaming behind Closed Doors,* 2015. She has recorded and studied more than 20 000 prophetic dreams, visions, and supernatural visitations. She founded and wrote the curriculum for **The Prophetic Path Dream Summit**, which teaches the prophetically inclined how to tap into the power of dreams.

Dwelling Places WORLDWIDE
A Publisher of Books & Letters
Amazon.com, BarnesandNoble.com
and other online outlets

I Waltzed with God the Morning of Genesis
Romancing God: The Divine Love Affair, Volumes 1-8
Romancing God: Memoirs of a Worshipper, Volumes 1-8
Stokestown: Dreaming behind Closed Doors
The River God Runs through Her: Praise for an unlikely Champion
Pastoral Letters: The Essential Collection
Studies in Prayer, Volumes 1-8
Tell Me Your Truth, I'll Sell You My Lie: behind the Veil of Santa Claus
The Night before Christ in the Battle for Christmas
Behind Enemy Lines: Strategist Weapons of Spiritual Warfare Sleep
Dream Sleep, Dream, become: Understanding the World You Dream
God, I'm Here and I 'm Colored: The National Debate on Race & Equality
Feat Songs of Protest and National Pride
The Hurt Café; How to Have Breakdown without Going Crazy

Coming Soon!!!

Chronicles of a Woman: An Epic Celebration of Woman in Full
Titles in Series Include the following

Woman of God become Thyself
Dead Woman Dancing on Her Grave: Unstoppable
The Dear John Reader: Rituals of Disclosure in Love and Emotional Emancipation
Rhapsody for September: Love Letters
The River God Runs through Her: Praise for An Unlikely Champion
Woman in a Jar: Narratives of an Imperfect Sanity
The Hurt Café: How to Have a Breakdown without Going Crazy
The Hurt Café, Volume 2: Narratives of Abuse and the Abdication of Shame
The Hurt Café, Volume 3: Healing for Wounded Warriors
The autobiography of Poverty: My Life in Poem
That Summer in London Where Love Found Me
First Lady, Last Victim
Angela of Gods: A Sister's Tribute to An Unsung Activist
The Gift of Flesh
Stokestown: Dreaming Behind Closed Doors

www.ingramcontent.com/pod-product-compliance
Lightning Source LLC
Chambersburg PA
CBHW050103170426
43198CB00014B/2446